J.D. Spencer is a qualified international healer and counsellor, a trained yoga and meditation teacher, and food allergy specialist. She ran The Allergy and Natural Healing Centre in Somerset, Southern England, for 15 years. Whilst living in Southern Spain, she had several healing clinics along the coast in Andalucia, in Fuengirola, Arroyo de la Miel and Malaga. She had stands in all the Alternative Medicine Exhibitions and was interviewed many times on television and radio.

To my wonderful family.

J.D. Spencer

CALAMARES AND CORRUPTION

A cautionary tale about buying property in Spain

AUSTIN MACAULEY PUBLISHERS™

LONDON · CAMBRIDGE · NEW YORK · SHARJAH

A CIP catalogue record for this title is available from the British Library.

ISBN 9781528939508 (Paperback)
ISBN 9781528939515 (Kindle e-book)
ISBN 9781528969963 (ePub e-book)

www.austinmacauley.com

First Published (2019)
Austin Macauley Publishers Ltd
25 Canada Square
Canary Wharf
London
E14 5LQ

I am very grateful to all the staff at Austin Macauley for bringing this book into publication and for all their care and attention. I have found all the staff very kind, patient and helpful.

Synopsis

This book involves endless dramas concerning the purchase of a ruined house in a remote mountain village in Andalucía, southern Spain. I bought it within 5 days of seeing an advert in a magazine. We owned the house for 20 years and lived there for 8 years. This book will be fascinating to thousands of expats living there and those who have returned to the UK or those who have holiday homes.

After rebuilding it for 6 years into a beautiful 6-bedroom house, my husband and I moved there as a family with two daughters, our horse and boxer dog, leaving our son behind. After 6 months, our marriage of 26 years collapsed and my husband returned to England. Heartbroken and on my own with two children, I was left to fend with the mayor of the village. He began his campaign to steal our land, with plans to build another house in our garden, even though we had legal documents.

After 3 years of fighting him together with my lawyer, an unexpected ally arrived on the scene—a Spanish friend who had a bookshop selling legal books to lawyers. He and I embarked on a massive onslaught against the mayor and the town hall and uncovered a huge amount of corruption. We took the mayor to court several times and ended up in all the major national newspapers. We received death threats and were spat on. Seven of our cats were poisoned.

There was also great excitement about my work as a healer. I went out on television as part of a film about our village and a few days later, queues of people were waiting in the street to see me. With so much work, I was able to open several clinics along the coast and over the years also taught yoga and English and rented rooms to students. Eventually, I managed to also set up my 2 pottery kilns and 2 wheels and made and exhibited pottery.

My youngest daughter almost died of an illness which is rarer in Spain than leprosy, called leishmania; it is transmitted by a sand fly from an infected dog. She was some weeks in an isolation unit in hospital. My other daughter worked training horses at Spanish riding stables with 65 horses.

We met many fascinating people, including the late Prince Pierre Raymond Doan Vinh, the last husband of the Woolworths heiress Barbara Hutton, Leonardo, the lead singer of Los Paraguayos, the late Lonnie Donegan and Ronnie Knight— before he gave himself up to the police and went to jail. We also met the late Phil Lynott, lead singer of the band Thin Lizzy.

Tired of the struggle against corruption, the court cases, battles and hostility within our village, we returned to the UK after 8 years, and then it took 4 more years to sell the property. Happily, not long after we left, encouraged by our efforts and prolonged struggle, the village people finally mustered some much-needed courage and offloaded the mayor after his 28-year reign of hell.

A Terrible Shock

After a harrowing drive up the narrow mountain road, with hairpin bends and sheer drops on both sides with no barriers, it was a great relief when the taxi pulled up at the top of the village. My 15-year-old son jumped out and ran off down the street, across the square and then headed down the steep hill to our house. Having seen the photos, he knew his way. I paid off the driver and looked around at the medieval village nestled in a dip in the mountains of southern Spain, its huddled houses with strange, curving Moorish walls, sun baked and whitewashed, dazzling my eyes. Tiny uneven cobbled streets with alleyways leading off into steep walkways, pots of red geraniums clinging to the walls everywhere, a bright blue sky and heavenly sunshine made the place quite magical. I slowly walked down the street, taking in that enchanting scene of utter delight. I crossed the square in front of the massive church, which only serviced less than 100 people and headed down to the house.

We tried the key in the lock, but the front door wouldn't budge. Seeing us struggling, a couple of neighbours came over to offer help. Someone else came along and told us there had been a storm, which had damaged our roof. What confronted us was hard to believe. A scene of utter devastation greeted us. The entire roof was on the floor. Wooden joists piled high, every beam and almost every roof tile smashed to pieces, it was about two feet deep in rubble. The beams, rubble and broken tiles covered every inch of the floor and were jammed up to the inside of the door and short of smashing the door down to get in, we had had to painstakingly try to inch it open enough to get a hand round to start shoving stuff aside. It had taken four of us two hours to get inside the house. As the roof had been perfectly alright 18 months previously, and had stood there for at least 100 years, it seemed impossible that such a thing could have happened.

11

We were too stunned to take it in. I was extremely upset for my son, who had been so excited about coming here and we had been looking forward to half camping in the house for a week. What to do at that point was totally beyond me. It was many years later that we found out the dreadful and appalling truth of that devastation. Looking back, I realise how utterly naïve I was to have fallen in love with what I thought was paradise.

A Crazy Week

Eighteen months earlier, my husband Jack and I had had a squabble and weren't speaking. It was a freezing cold Monday in January. A copy of my favourite monthly health magazine had arrived and I was leafing through to find the advertisement I put in there on a regular basis. Idly looking at the classified ads, I saw a house for sale in southern Spain—oh my God, it was so ridiculously cheap that it was obviously a hovel. Jack and I didn't talk on Tuesday but having made up by Wednesday morning, I gingerly showed him the advert and asked him if we should buy it. He smiled sweetly and said why not, sounded like a good idea. I was pretty dumbfounded, such an amenable bloke, I could hardly believe my ears.

"Give them a ring," he said. I rang Wednesday night, nobody was there. I rang Thursday and got someone in the evening. She said there had been a mistake in the advert; the price was quite a lot more. She said she had had lots of enquiries and was leaving for Spain Saturday morning and that various people wanted to fly out and look at it. She said the house was very old and up in the hills, a few miles inland from the coast in a village which at that time was totally unpronounceable for me. No mention of mountains. It sounded interesting.

"I want to buy it over the phone, then," I said.

"You cannot do that," she said. "Nobody can buy a house over the phone."

"I've just done it," I said. "We will travel over with you Saturday morning." She was catching a plane to Malaga at 6 a.m. from Manchester. We were living in Somerset.

I rushed down the garden to tell Jack. We had a business on the premises, a workshop where Jack bought and sold cars, did repair work but mostly did bodywork.

"We will have to fly to Spain on Saturday morning," I told him excitedly.

"I can't go," he said. "I have far too much work, you will have to go."

I said, "I cannot possibly buy a house in Spain on my own! And what about the children?"

"Get going, I will cope with everything here," he said.

My passport was out of date. I got up Friday morning, went to Taunton to organise a temporary passport and a flight to Malaga. I sat for 3 hours in the travel agent's office whilst they tried to get me on the same flight out of Manchester as the woman. The only flight I could get on left 3 hours later, at 9 a.m. I had to leave pretty quickly to get up to Manchester. I left by bus at lunchtime.

I had no time to think straight, no time to tell anyone, not even my sisters, brother or closest friends. The only call I made was to a colleague to take over my yoga classes. It was utter madness. I was on my way to Spain to buy a house I had never seen, on a mad impulse, with the full support of my husband, all in the space of 3 days. If I had only known what was ahead of me.

The bus arrived in Manchester in the late afternoon and I had to spend the night there. It was a pretty airport, and I was given a bed for the night, which greatly surprised me. I was up at about 4 a.m., as I had arranged to meet the lady in question, and that was my first shock.

She was a young punk with the wildest hair I had ever seen, an electric shock of gelled porcupine spikes, bright blue and sprayed with silver, dressed in black leather and studs from head to toe. She was surrounded by a group of other punks, all about 20 years old, and I had the awful feeling I was being taken for a ride, that it was all a con and I had fallen for it. How could a young slip of a girl like this own a house in Spain?

I was about to part with the only savings we had at that time, and now I had serious doubts about the whole thing. Fear gripped me. I rang my husband.

"I'm going to pull out," I said. "I think we are being conned; the girl is a punk, only about 22 years old. How can she possibly own a house in Spain?"

He was laid back about it, but then he was laid back about everything.

Well, it was my own fault, rushing into it. There I was, and I decided I would go ahead with the flight, having got that far. At one point, I managed to question her wild-looking companions whilst she was occupied, to ask if she really did own that house. They assured me she did, but I was hardly convinced.

Rebecca flew out of Manchester at 6 a.m. and I left at 9 a.m. and she met me in Malaga airport. She was with a companion, a guy dressed in black leather with pitch black sunglasses—I never did get to see his eyes. They drove me through Malaga, which looked astonishing, hot and dry, exotic and busy, with beautiful palm trees, flowers, and then on out onto the coast road with its delightful sandy beaches and blue seas. It all looked delightful. We eventually turned inland and began climbing up. The road was appalling, full of potholes, narrow and barely more than a track with hardly a place to pass and terrifying hairpin bends. The hills she had mentioned were in fact mountains, and I was petrified. There were sheer drops over both sides. They pointed out a couple of cars way down at the bottom of the valley; people had driven over the edge and obviously hadn't lived to tell the tale. Five people had died in one car alone. Not what I needed to hear at that moment.

The landscape was utterly beautiful and I fell in love immediately. In fact, I was ecstatic and beside myself with excitement. I tried to stay outwardly calm and unmoved. After all, I didn't want to seem too keen, or the price might have gone up even more. I didn't believe the magazine put the price in wrong, I thought she had had a few calls and had decided she could get more for it. Who could blame her?

My experience of Spain at that time was very limited. We had been to Majorca lots of times because my brother had several travel agencies and often offered us free flights at the last minute. The only time I had been to mainland Spain was aged 19, to Barcelona. I went with a South African girl of 33, who was mad about architecture and spent the whole time raving about Antoni Gaudí. He was the extraordinary artist, architect and designer who built the most remarkable and beautiful buildings, most famously the Sagrada Familia, the strange and fascinating cathedral which is still not completed. Although I loved the buildings we saw that he had designed, and they certainly fascinate me now, at that time, aged 19, I was rather more interested in the black haired and beautiful Spanish men.

Barcelona was stunning and very foreign, with that smell Spain had, all of its own. We took a taxi from the airport and told the driver to take us to a cheap hotel in the middle of Barcelona. We arrived at 2 a.m. and I still vividly remember the reek of garlic on the porter's breath, which nearly knocked us over as he took us up a few floors in a tiny wobbly ancient lift. He asked for our passports and wanted to keep them overnight, and I ended up wrestling with him to get mine back. When we woke up in the morning and looked out of the window, we looked out onto a huge piece of wasteland, covered in rubbish and teeming with dozens of rats.

A Terrifying Road

Now we twisted up around endless hairpin bends, whilst I tried desperately to keep my eyes ahead. We arrived at a kind of plateau and looked down at the village. It was a spectacular sight with the Sierra Nevada Mountains in the distance. We wound our way down into the stunning village with whitewashed houses snuggled together, a beautiful square and the biggest church I had ever seen. We carried on through the village, past tiny houses and around very tight bends and out the other side and to the house. It was an end terrace of three on quite a steep hill. The house was at the top of the hill, with the enormous church right behind it.

It was a house in the most beautiful village I had ever seen and I really didn't care what it was like inside. It was mine and I had to have it. A piece of real estate in Andalucía and we could afford it—just barely.

At this point, it is interesting to note that the roof happily sat there.

Inside, there was a large sitting room with gorgeous old earthenware tiles on the floor, another room which had been used as a bedroom and out the back were a couple of rooms, one with the roof fallen in and the other had a roof which dipped wildly. Children had made a camp on top of it. No bathroom, no kitchen, no water, no electricity. It had at one time been a very large house with all the rooms at the back intact and with an upstairs, but it had gradually fallen down over the years, with the previous owners unable to repair it.

There was a garden out the back, completely overgrown with a fig tree. A mountain of rubbish was piled high in the middle of the garden—rubbish of every description, all evidently thrown by the next-door neighbour. It was disgusting. I was worried about what my husband would think of it. I wasn't worried about the fact that the house was a near hovel and the back of it had fallen down.

Rebecca seemed to be known by all the neighbours and they greeted her affectionately. She had a chat with the neighbours next door and asked them if they would be kind enough to remove the rubbish for us after we had gone. I paid them what she asked; it was ironic, seeing it was them who had thrown it there. At least I hoped they would get the message and stop chucking it there. By the look of their garden, which was also full of rubbish, I didn't hold out a lot of hope.

I had, however, by this time fallen in love with Spain and everything and everybody Spanish; the neighbours all seemed delightful and the village was enchanting. I was utterly captivated by it all and in a state of euphoria. I was told that the only English people in the village were a very eccentric couple; the lady never went out because she was alcoholic, they kept parrots and a monkey slept on their bed.

Roughing it wouldn't bother us; we had done the same thing in Somerset. We'd left the rat race in London, gone to the Bahamas to work for a year, saved up enough money to buy a one-up-one-down cottage in Somerset with a broken staircase, no electricity, no water, no bathroom, no kitchen—just an old wooden shed on the side. We spent 8 years building a beautiful house ourselves, raising it 3 feet off the ground because we were flooded 10 times in the first year we lived there, a couple of feet of water in the house at a time. When everybody else was going to the coast for the weekend, we were mixing cement and going up and down ladders with breeze blocks.

Looking at the roof now, all I knew was it was sitting there looking solid, with open beams and tiles, no sign of leaks. It looked fine to me. We never did believe in surveys and for that price, the thought didn't even enter my mind. I tried to barter but she wasn't having any of it. "I'll take it," I said.

So there I was, 5 days after seeing the advert, almost the owner of a house in Spain. She knew of a lawyer in Malaga, and after a bite to eat in the local bar of very smelly sheep's cheese, which tasted like the sheep itself, crusty bread, olives and a glass of wine, we set off.

The lawyer in Malaga wasn't there. We spent every day from Saturday until Wednesday waiting for him. I found out later that the man was a notorious crook. He had gone to Belgium with his wife on holiday and his wife had had an accident and was in hospital. He didn't know when they would be home. His office staff kept ringing him but by the Wednesday, we realised we had to find somebody else in a hurry since I had a ticket to return on the Saturday.

The girl knew another lawyer. We got there at around 5.30 p.m. It had been a tense few days waiting, but now it would be alright, I told myself. The lawyer even spoke perfect English. I had started learning Spanish when I was 16, at the same time as studying A levels in French and German. Then I did a further 2-year intensive course at 22 with a group of Japanese people at Mitsubishi in London, where I was working and also learning Japanese. We had employed somebody from the Spanish Embassy to teach a group of us and now I couldn't even remember how to order a cup of coffee.

No Deeds

The lawyer seemed very pleasant. He asked the girl for her deeds, the Escritura. She didn't have any. I was so naïve, it hadn't occurred to me that she wouldn't have any deeds. Who doesn't have deeds of their house? He then looked at me and strongly advised me not to buy the property. We were both devastated. I desperately wanted it; she desperately wanted to sell it. She wasn't living in it; she was living on the coast in someone's house while they were away. She hadn't got two beans to rub together. She had bought the house on the spur of the moment, borrowed the money from her brother and he was demanding the money back.

She had a simple contract and on that contract was the name of a previous owner whose family had lived in the house for 40 years. He lived in a village nearby. The lawyer said, "Let's go and see him and see if we can start proceedings to make a proper Escritura."

It was further up in the mountains, so once again we made a trek upwards round more hair-raising bends. The village was built on the side of the mountain and was mostly one narrow street. We parked the car and set off to find our man. There was my friend with her blue and silver spiked hair standing on end, glitter all over her face and dressed in leather from head to toe, with high-heeled black boots covered in studs. There was the lawyer, a most handsome, well-dressed young man and quite delightful and myself, a blond in high heels and short skirt. As we climbed up the deserted cobbled street, people spilled out of their doorways to stare. We were directed to the house and invited in. It was a tiny house, bare but for a few chairs and a table. The gentleman we were looking for was out on his land, working. His wife made us very welcome and a son was summoned, and we all set off to look for him.

We walked for an hour in the hot sunshine, stumbling over rocky terrain, walking through scraggy bushes and over hills, quite a feat in stupid high heeled shoes. The views and hills were breath-taking. It was heaven to me. We finally arrived at a tiny hut in the middle of nowhere, where a man and his sons were working. Grapes were piled high, goats were grazing. It was enchanting. We introduced ourselves and were offered the most beautiful, sweetest home-made wine I had ever tasted, made of raisins, known as vino dulce.

We sat around on the ground whilst they discussed the matter, all of which was over my head, and as my cup was refilled, I became merrier by the minute. Sergio then told us he was finished for the day and would return with us to his home. We set off on the return trek, and Sergio invited us in, insisting on offering us more wine, whilst his wife pressed us to have bread, meats and cheeses. It seemed that after some discussion, he was willing to help and we had the thumbs up that the paperwork would be OK. I was ecstatic. The family were so kind and hospitable and became close friends of ours. They had several children and kept dozens of goats, and there were lots of cats and dogs all over the place.

When we got back down to the coast, I rang my husband and in a drunken state informed him that we had a house in Spain and it was utterly lovely, perfectly in order and didn't need any work doing to it at all. I somehow omitted to mention that the whole of the back of the house had fallen down, there were piles of rubble all around it, some at least 6 feet high, it had no facilities whatsoever, and in fact it was a hovel. When I woke up the next day with a hangover, I realised that my husband would get a shock when he saw the photographs. What the hell had I done? He'd sounded so happy about it, I didn't have the heart to ring him again and tell him the truth, I thought it could wait until I got home; I still had lots left to do in any case.

I had been staying in different places, the first night in Malaga. They had taken me and dropped me off right in the centre and booked me into a room. It was late, but I decided to take a walk and have a look round. I set off at 10 p.m. and walked down to what looked like a park. I was approached by various men which scared me, so I headed back. I later discovered that it was quite a dodgy place for pickups.

I got back to the hostel, as it was called; my room was up on the second floor. There was a very shifty-eyed character sitting on the stairs and I had to walk past him. I had been told to put the strap of my shoulder bag firmly over my head and resting on the opposite shoulder. I then went into a small general sitting room for everyone and was able to talk to a Moroccan, as I could still remember my French.

I hadn't been there 5 minutes when an almighty commotion started in the lobby. Two Australian girls were coming up the stairs and the creepy guy had grabbed one of them, she had had her purse round her neck. She was struggling fiercely, both girls were screaming, men came running and they had quite a job to pin the guy to the floor. He was big and fighting back and had a mate with him who must have been hiding somewhere. The second guy got away and ran off. I was rooted to the floor with fear. One of the men shouted at me to ring the police, and I picked up the phone and then realised I had no idea how to do it. Somebody else called them and they arrived within 5 minutes, whilst 4 men had their work cut out trying to sit on this guy and keep him still. I found I was shaking like a leaf. That was my first night in Malaga, and it was pretty unnerving. I didn't get much sleep.

After that, the girl put me up here and there. She had a system going whereby if people were away, she offered to move in, live there and take care of their property for them. The owners were happy and she lived rent free. She had long since given up trying to rough it in the mountains.

The next morning, I woke up in some villa she was using on the coast. There was a knock on my bedroom door and into my room stepped someone I hadn't seen before. In front of me stood an overweight, frumpy girl with short, lank and straight brown hair stuck to the sides of her face and no makeup. She was wearing an awful, dowdy towel dressing gown. She then asked me if I would like a cup of tea in a voice I recognised. Here was my friend without her disguise! I gaped in wonder.

We had breakfast; she gave me a bowl of huge delicious raisins with muesli. Then, in fascination, I watched her in the bathroom getting herself ready for the day. It took an hour, putting on makeup, painting silver marks on her face, doing the hair blue and silver and standing it on end in big spikes with piles of gel. Then all the clobber went on, black leather covered in studs, black boots, loads of bracelets and at the end of it, the dowdy mouse had been transformed into a spectacular sight. I wondered if her Spanish boyfriend had ever seen her in the mornings.

Time to Get Started

When I got back to Somerset and had the photos printed, I had to apologise to Jack. He looked quite disappointed to find that it wasn't after all an up-together cottage as I had described. It didn't, however, appear to deter him any and two months later, he packed a big bag of tools, put in 2 cartons of fruit juice and some clothes and off he went to Malaga for 2 weeks, with intentions of seeing what needed doing.

Before he left, I made him promise that he would not make any attempt to try and get to the village other than by taxi; there were no buses and he couldn't possibly walk the 10 kilometres from the coast. He got on a bus from Malaga; put his bag of tools which weighed a ton into the luggage compartment at the back of the bus as instructed by the driver. He asked for the village, the driver indicated he would let him know when he got there and then forgot about him. About 15 miles past the end of the road where he should have got off, he asked the driver again. The driver held up his arms in horror and told him he had to go all the way back again.

He got off the bus and the driver drove off before he could get his tool bag out of the boot. Jack ran like a mad thing after the bus, just got hold of the handle of the boot, and running at a pace, managed to get the boot open and grab his bag by the handle, gave it a yank and landed in the middle of the road on his back with his bag on top of him. He then waited for a bus to go back and he was dropped off at the bottom of the mountain, not a taxi in sight. He walked 10 kilometres up the mountain with a very heavy bag of tools. It took him several hours. He drank both cartons of fruit juice on the way. When he reached the plateau and it was mostly downhill from there, the baker came along and gave him a lift for the rest of the way.

He didn't ring me for 11 days and I lost half a stone of weight worrying about him. He had arrived at the village, found the house and was sitting on a wall surveying the scene and the only Englishman in the village came along, introduced himself and took him in, where he was utterly pampered and taken care of, by him and his wife; he was fed and watered. They helped him organise building materials and made a fantastic start on the whole project. They employed several men and began by rebuilding the back part of the house, getting it up to ceiling level, ready to go up another floor. He had made contact with the local lorry driver, who brought up the materials. By the time he finally phoned, I was feeling frantic. I was greatly relieved that he was OK and doing well and had managed to organise the work involved.

In order to get planning permission for the building work to be done, the mayor had informed me, when I had gone over on an earlier visit with my children, that I had to draw him a plan and pay him some money and the building could go ahead. I had a tiny notebook in my bag at the time and I sat down in the street and drew a drawing of a house as I imagined it would look like upon completion, on a tiny piece of paper. I then went along to the town hall, handed it over, and paid the equivalent of £5 and I was given an equally small piece of paper with a stamp on it, and that was my permission. The only comment he made was that he expected me to put red terracotta tiles on the roof, which it already had. I remember my English neighbour went a bit crazy when I told her about the transaction and started shouting that the mayor had ripped me off by charging me £5!

So a good start had been made on the house. There was almost total unemployment in the village and a lot of the men wanted to get the work that we were creating. Out of about 100 people, a few had goats, one or two had a bit of land, and there was the odd rare bit of building work. There was only one car in the entire village, owned by our English neighbour. He gave people lifts up and down the mountain but had to be careful, as the taxi drivers wanted the work and he could have got into trouble. There was a school bus that went down in the morning and came back in the afternoon and people hopped on that.

I took the children over to Malaga a couple of times, and we camped in the house. As soon as we arrived, it would fill up with children. They often arrived in the evening when we had lit candles and we had a lot of fun with them. They were trying to teach us Spanish. There was no furniture, just a couple of concrete benches on either side of a fireplace, which we used as beds and chairs. They sat all over the floor.

One time I took my daughter Sandra over for two weeks and stayed on the coast in Benalmadena for several days to attend an Alternative Medicine Convention, attended by 500 doctors and therapists from all over the world. I am a healer and food allergy therapist and was running the Allergy and Natural Healing Centre in Somerset. We stayed in a delightful room above a restaurant, with a pretty sitting room full of bamboo furniture and a veranda overlooking the busy street. We were fortunate to be serenaded every evening by a singer who played guitar.

The conference was immensely interesting for me, with lectures on all aspects of natural medicine. It was organised by people from Singapore, and it was a pleasure to meet so many inspiring characters. Sandra was about 14 at the time and throughout the day, she sat through as many lectures on acupuncture as she could stand and eventually spent her time by the hotel pool. I gave a lecture on food allergies and vitamin and mineral deficiencies and found that 3 glasses of champagne beforehand gave me the much needed confidence to do so and helped alleviate my nerves no end.

Back at the house with no means to wash any clothes, we would join the women from the village at the local wash sinks which had been built in the hillside alongside a natural spring which came down from the higher mountains. Nobody had washing machines at that time. Several concrete sinks had been built alongside each other on slightly different levels with holes in and old socks to use as plugs. It took me a while to get the hang of it, as I kept flooding it all because I wasn't plugging the right holes. I would take our washing there, scrub away in cold water, get home and hang the washing out to find it was all just as dirty as before. At least we got to know all the women in the village, and I spent many a happy hour there chattering.

Many years later, a group of us had this spring water analysed and it was found to be almost totally pure. People would come from far and wide to collect it, the owner of a shop on the coast would drive up and fill dozens of bottles and then sell it in his shop. It ran almost the entire year, apart from very severe droughts and a neighbour had organised the excess water to pour into his land to water his vegetables and fruit trees. All the villagers used it as drinking water and for cooking, and it was infinitely safer than the tap water which the mayor would 'purify' by pouring in piles of bleach. One year, he poured in far too much, and half the people got diarrhoea.

Back to the Destruction

When we then didn't return to the house for a period of about 18 months, as I have said, my son and I were horrified to find the entire roof of the house on the floor. It was such a terrible shock. When I had bought the house, the tiles were all in place and in good order. Jack had noticed 3 of the beams had been pretty wormy and had said that a small section had looked a bit dubious. To find the entire roof down, smashed to pieces, tiles all broken, beams beyond repair and smashed into pieces, with not a square foot of floor to stand on, was truly shocking. With talk of storm damage, what other answer could there be? I had to accept it, as there seemed no alternative.

It was obviously totally uninhabitable, even for camping, and I was at a loss to know what to do. It was immensely disappointing, but we were thankfully rescued by the English neighbours who saw us out in the street and invited us in. They offered us beds and food and suggested a very reasonable amount as a contribution, for which we were extremely grateful. It turned out that this lady had been an alcoholic for many years and almost never left the house. With us there, she was coaxed to go out and we all enjoyed some very nice trips out and about together.

It wasn't for many years after we had been living there that we discovered the awful truth about our roof. Our next-door neighbour and his 3 sons had laid on top of the roof and smashed the whole lot in. Another neighbour who became a good friend saw them doing it. They had no work. They knew we would hear about it and would rush over and employ them to start work again. They obviously thought we were rolling in money. We were a working family with 3 children and trying to save up batches of money to transfer to Spain to pay for it all. The day I found out the truth, many years later, I was so angry I was beside myself, because many more awful things had happened by then. I wrote them a letter telling them I knew about it, with a few comments about how they would receive their comeuppance with the laws of karma. They tore it into shreds and posted it back through my letter box.

As for the roof on the floor, there was nothing I could do about it at that time. Naturally, as soon as Jack heard about it, he was over, employing all the neighbours and that was, after all, what they wanted. The men there pretty much queued up for work, vying with one another, and we had to be very diplomatic, trying to employ men from different families but especially our nearest neighbours. The rates of pay for men at that time were ridiculously low, but then so was the cost of living. It has certainly changed now. In the early days of the project, we were paying men the equivalent of £7.00 per day; this seemed to go up each time we went out there.

Although Jack wanted to be hands on with all parts of the building work, he decided to delegate some it out and we arranged for money to go over and our dear English neighbours employed some guys to do building work. A lot of money was being sent to Spain and a lot of work was getting done. We were rebuilding it to its original size and it ended up with 6 very large bedrooms upstairs, a big sitting room, huge kitchen, a lovely big bathroom and a study. We had further plans for a garage and workshop at the side and a further bathroom.

Eventually, we felt it was getting too much work for our English neighbour, as he was getting on in years and there was a lot of organising to do. We transferred the responsibility to our neighbour Joaquin, who had been doing a lot of the actual building work. He was a very honest and lovely man, and we became very good friends with him and all his family. One time we sent him £3000 and I was then out there some weeks later. He told me that he had been up all night because he couldn't account for £34, he had receipts and accounts for everything. I told him it didn't matter, I wasn't worried about £34. I told him to forget it. No, he spent another night up, going through it and the following morning, came over with all the papers—it had been a miscalculation. He insisted that I went through it all with him to confirm the mistake.

We had a lot of fun with his family and went out together on many trips. Joaquin loved to come out with us in our hire car and show us around, taking us to remote villages in the back of beyond. I was told that Joaquin's wife Maria was a gypsy. She didn't look like a gypsy, and I didn't care one way or the other. She was always very sweet to us and welcomed us into her home any time. When she died many years later, I was astonished to open my front door and see about 600 gypsies filling the entire village on the day of her funeral.

A guy from the next village, a roofer, put the roof on in our absence and did a good job, we used what was left of the old original tiles, those that weren't broken from the destruction plus new ones. It was much to our dismay that not long after that when we were visiting a relative of his, we discovered that he had lost a hand in a firework incident. He was supplied with an excellent false hand and unless you knew, you would not have noticed it. His days of building, however, were over. Fireworks were lethal in Spain then and did not appear to be regulated in any way. A friend of mine bought lots of illegal fireworks from Malaga market when she stayed with me for her children and despite my horror and pleadings not to, she then took them home on a plane.

The house was now pretty spacious; we had made it very interesting, keeping old doors, putting in open beams up and down. Jack built the kitchen cupboards from some lovely old panelled wood he found and we inlaid tiny colourful old Andalucían tiles on the worktops. We had a lovely house and a pretty garden. It was delightful. It had taken us 6 years to complete.

The first and second times I ever went up to the village in a taxi, I more or less hid in the back seat, cowering with fright. I presumed that this house would only ever be a holiday home because I thought I could never cope with going up and down that road. On our visits there, I often caught the school bus up. One day, we met a car coming down. The driver stopped, paralysed with fear and unable to move. Everybody on the bus piled out, the man was obviously a visitor and hadn't expected to meet a bus. It took 20 minutes to calm him down and help him move so that we could get past. There were sheer drops on the mountain roads with no barriers. A huge basura or rubbish tip burned constantly, day and night, rubbish blown all over the roads, it was hazardous to drive by it as the smoke was so thick, you couldn't see. People used to drive in there and rummage through the rubbish for bargains, with rats running all over the place.

The Big Decision

The momentous day came when we decided to move there. We had been having some serious marital problems. Jack had given up smoking, which brought on a mid-life crisis; he was in a bad state for a long time. Frankly, it was a nightmare. He withdrew into himself, rejected me and refused to have any help or treatment, insisting there was nothing wrong with him. His whole demeanour and attitude changed and it was very difficult for me to cope with. As the business took up almost all of his time and was pretty stressful, we thought we would retire, sell our house, invest the money and live on the interest, which was very high at the time. We had 3 children, a horse, 2 goats and a boxer dog. We decided everybody would be going.

Our son Will was 19 and refused to go. Our eldest daughter Sandra who was 16 had hysterics and sulked for weeks, crying. My husband said we could not take the horse, the goats, the piano or the pottery. Nobody in their right mind would take a horse and two goats, he said. Sandra and I went to our local stables and asked them if they could sell our horse for us. We then both cried for a week and couldn't sleep. I told Jack, if we went, the horse went with us. She was one of the family—the goats too. He caved in.

He wanted me to sell my piano and all my pottery equipment. I then told him I couldn't live without my piano or my pottery. When I say pottery, I mean 2 wheels and 2 kilns, mountains of equipment, sacks of clay and hundreds of pots. My piano had belonged to my mother, and I had had it all my life. My pottery and piano are part of who I am and I was not prepared to leave any of it. My mother had taken all of us 4 children to piano lessons every week for years. I had lessons for 8 years since the age of 6. It was the first time I suddenly had doubts about our relationship. It seemed my husband didn't understand who I was. Without my horse, pots and piano, I wouldn't have existed. Jack was taking all his tools of the business, which was a thriving garage, including a big compressor. We also had lots of antiques we wanted to keep, and it was all becoming a bit daunting.

The paperwork to take the horse, goats and boxer dog took me a year, back and forth to the Ministry of Agriculture. It took us a year to sell our house as the collapse had just started and we were asking too much money. Then the worst blow of all—our 2 goats failed their blood tests, with only a few days to go before we were due to leave. It was a major catastrophe for me. We had had them since they were a few weeks old twins. They were 9 years old. They were both perfectly well. We were very fortunate indeed that a delightful family who bought our house kindly decided to take them on and looked after them fantastically well. They lived for another 6 years, extremely well cared for. They were both 15 when they died. I visited them often, which was always traumatic because it upset me so much. It distressed me terribly that we had to leave them behind.

We Set Off

We eventually arrived to live there in the summer of 1989. The summers down in southern Spain are immensely hot, being so close to Morocco. We had been very tired of the English climate of rain and more rain and we were looking forward to some hot weather. Some blue and yellow instead of green and grey. The immense heat did, however, bring with it unbelievable problems.

The journey there was quite eventful, with our horse Tammy in a box behind us. When we arrived at the ferry, the officials were waiting for us; they spoke to each other through their intercoms.

"The horse has arrived, the horse has arrived." We were given a special place on the top deck so Tammy could have fresh air. Every half an hour, an official visited us to see if she was alright. I was very impressed with their concern. Nobody enquired after us. Passengers kept asking us if we couldn't go on holiday without our horse. Sandra was extremely nervous and spent the whole journey in the horse box. In fact, Tammy was perfectly fine. We were stopped when we arrived at the French port and asked to pull over to one side where a few inspectors checked the horse box, the main inspector informing us proudly that he had a horse and his was much bigger than ours. We had piles of papers to show them in French and Spanish relating to Tammy and our boxer dog Saul, which were all satisfactory.

We were not quite so fine during the trip down through France, however, when we decided to stop and let Tam out for a walk and to have a rest. We turned off the motorway and found a remote country spot with lots of fresh grass and a suitable lay-by with masses of open land. She, however, had had enough of it in the box after about 14 hours. As we were letting her out, she reared up and broke away. Sandra fell on the floor, and Tammy managed to step on her as she galloped off and over the hills, a speck in the distance, heading towards the motorway. After an hour or so of frantic running about with no success and all of us pretty worn out and frustrated, Jack was jokingly threatening to leave her there or take her to the local meat factory if we ever caught her.

We stopped some people who were driving past and asked them to ring the police to come and help us. By the time the police arrived, we had managed to get hold of her. It had taken us 2 and a half hours. We had a double horsebox and had to unload piles of hay and feed that we had packed into one side, get her in and repack all the stuff back in again. The police were very pleasant and helpful. Tammy had to stay in after that. We weren't going to risk any more dramas. Saul also got very fed up with the travelling, and even though we stopped several times to

28

give us all a break, we had a job to get him back in the car afterwards.

It was a long journey down through France with mile upon mile of wheat, sunflowers and grapes. We got safely through the Spanish customs with all the necessary paperwork, which was a huge relief. The lush green growth of northern Spain with beautiful forests, hills and rivers eventually gave way to endless miles of wheat, which went on for so long I found it unnerving. We seemed to be lost in a wilderness with no sign of civilisation. Once past Madrid with its nightmare jungle of junctions and signs, we headed south on what appeared to be a good road on the map, but was in fact an incredibly mountainous journey which we could have done without. It could not have been easy for Tammy, with one hairpin bend after another

I recall one extraordinarily high bridge over a river which we could see coming up from miles away, rather like the Clifton Suspension bridge in Bristol. I had to get in the back of the car and put my head under a pillow, as I have a horror of bridges. Many years later, when I was in that area again and the road over the bridge was closed, I was informed, much to my horror, that the bridge had collapsed.

I get very nervous driving over bridges. I'm sure it stems from my childhood when I was about 8 years old and I stood on a very high bridge in Yorkshire with my parents and uncle looking down a long way to the tops of oak trees. My uncle told us how my aunt had just jumped off and tried to kill herself. She landed into the top of a tree and managed to survive and was at that moment in hospital.

We finally arrived at the coastal junction where we would then turn off to climb up to the village. It was late at night and dark and as we turned off, we were shocked to discover that the road had disappeared because there was massive building work going on. There were no street lights and nothing but wasteland and piles of earth and we had no idea where to go or how to get out of that mess. At that point, Sandra burst into tears. She had been so brave dealing with Tammy for the whole journey with all its dramas, but that was the last straw. Out of nowhere appeared a man who waved us on with a torch and slowly led us through the dirt piles and mountains of bricks, until we once again joined the road we knew.

Here at Last

It was with great relief that we arrived at our village. The first thing we did was let Tammy out of the box to stretch her legs, she was quite stiff and very glad to get out. We held her very firmly this time. Sandra walked her up and down the roads to get her circulation going. It was about 11 o'clock and all the neighbours were still up and came out of their houses to greet us. It was very exciting and as we opened our front door, they all trooped in with us. We hadn't seen the last of the work that had been done, the laying of the all the floor tiles which I had bought on my last trip over, but obviously they all had, and they were anxious that we should like them. They didn't stay too long, as we were tired and needed to get organised. They hadn't met Tammy and there was much excitement in seeing her arrive. After giving her a good long walk, we settled her in the back garden with plenty of food and water and she was very relieved to be safely back on firm ground.

Our bathroom wasn't finished. All the pieces were fitted but not plumbed in, so we were still doing what we had to do in a bucket and burying it, and we rigged up a hose pipe in the fig tree for showers, using an empty washing up bottle with holes in which worked very well. The local boys would stand in the churchyard behind, hoping to spot us naked, so we had to shower with swimwear on. We urgently contacted a plumber and got the bathroom working within the first week, a great relief to us all.

Fortunately, the original walls of our house downstairs were about 2 feet thick and kept the house cool but as you opened the door to go out in the street, it was like opening an oven door where you are baking a pizza. Insects of every description descended on us, we had armies of ants coming in the back door, thousands of them in lines, and if you followed the lines, they went out over the hill. Flies were trying to get in everywhere.

Saul soon became covered in dreadful insects which I had never seen before. We found out they were ticks, disgusting and dangerous creatures that hooked themselves on to animals and humans. They then suck the blood and horrid greyish swellings balloon up. They spread disease. I was quite frantic, but a neighbour told us we could buy tick collars which prevented them biting the animal. Until we were able to get one, we had to pull them out with tweezers, which was not a good idea as the heads can be left in and cause infection. We had no stable at that time, and we had the horse tied up in the garden on a long rope under either the fig tree or the olive tree. We had brought several bales of hay and several sacks of feed with us to keep us going until we could find out where to buy it.

When we first bought the house, I had noticed a tiny olive tree had seeded itself right in the middle of the garden. It was only about 6 inches high. I was very pleased. By the time we moved there, it had grown into a substantial tree and afforded us and especially Tammy a lot of shelter. We hosed Tammy down twice a day in the heat under the olive tree—she loved it. As a result of receiving so much water, the tree grew to be the biggest olive tree I ever saw there, the black olives were just huge. I tried my best to harvest them. Most years they turned out well and others not. Everybody gave me different advice on how to preserve them.

I had had a struggle to keep the fig tree. Everybody had wanted to cut it down. It was very close to the back of the house and Jack and the men working for him all insisted it was useless, never had any fruit on it because it was so old and it was simply in the way. I stood firm. I had never owned a fig tree and I wasn't going to let anybody touch it. We argued about it lots of times, but I was adamant. They trimmed some branches in the end and I was very relieved. It grew to be the most fantastic tree you ever saw, absolutely laden with figs, they fell all over the garden, we gave bowls of them away, we froze them, we ate them raw, we cooked them and Tammy ate them. Fresh figs are superb and the tree gave us some very much needed extra shade. I have heard it said that you are blessed if you own a fig tree or an olive tree. Well, I felt we were all truly blessed with having one of each.

The first night there, we hardly slept a wink. We had been living in the country with hardly a neighbour in sight. All night, dogs howled and barked. The neighbours seemed to be up half the night talking and then up at the crack of dawn. Cockerels were crowing. I could not believe the noise. The first morning there, we got up, opened the front door and saw to our astonishment a group of young lads sitting on the wall opposite, waiting for us to appear. Well, it wasn't exactly all of us they were waiting for, but our 17-year-old daughter, a beautiful girl with white blond hair. At the time, she looked like a cross between a punk and the singer of Transvision Vamp. She had two pony tails, one on the top of her head and one on the back. She was wearing micro skirts and some pretty wild tops. Word had spread fast. My neighbours had never seen some of the boys; they had come over the hills. Every day was the same; they were waiting to get a glimpse of her, different boys from different places. It was very amusing but also very scary. Locking up my daughters until they were 30 seemed like an excellent idea.

The Annual Feria

We arrived in the middle of the annual feria. We had come the previous year and experienced the feria then. For a small village, we had the longest-lasting feria in southern Spain—it went on for 10 days. If you haven't seen a Spanish feria, you have really missed something. I became an addict. I dragged my daughters to every feria in the entire region for about 2 years until even I got tired of them. They start very late at night, everybody gets incredibly merry and dances all night long in the street. Coming from England, it was really intoxicating. In fact, the girl who had sold us the house was from Yorkshire, she had gone on holiday with her friend for 2 weeks, gone to a feria, danced in the streets every night and at the end of the fortnight, refused to go home. Her friend had to return alone and explain to the poor girl's mother that she wasn't coming back. She was 19. She urged me to go to a feria at the first opportunity.

Usually, the whole village turns out for the feria—young children, elderly relatives and everybody in between. Children play and stay out very late in Spain, they do not have the rules we have of sending them to bed at a certain time. Hours are kept late because it is the only time of the day when it is cool, it's hard to function at all during the intense heat of the day. There are inevitably a few problems in the ferias with people drinking too much. Wine is so plentiful and cheap. We once saw a young guy go up to another guy and evidently ask him for some money back that he had lent him. The two of them started a fight and then the next minute, several men started hitting each other and the entire thing turned into a brawl, with several men all knocking the hell out of each other.

The first night of the feria, walking back to our house, I was shocked to see about half a dozen men all peeing against the church wall, right there in the street. There was a foul stench. What with that and the ticks, much to the amusement of my English neighbour, I was wondering where on earth we had landed. Somerset seemed like another planet.

During the day, there were various events laid on for the children, races and games. One day, a lorry arrived and several men unloaded a young bull, grappling roughly with it, screaming at it. They shoved it into the square, which had been barricaded off so it couldn't escape. We stayed a while in the hope that it may be some harmless fun, but they proceeded to torture the terrified animal, stabbing it with several knives whilst everybody looked on laughing and baying for its blood and suffering. We walked away in disgust. Later in the day, I saw the pools of blood on the stones of the square left for all to see.

Big Drama with Tammy

On about the third night of the feria, Jack had gone home at about 3 a.m. and had been woken up by our neighbour next door. Our horse Tammy had been tied up to our fig tree on a long rope and she had fallen down into the next door neighbour's garden, a drop of about 8 feet. Jack came running up to the square to get me and I rushed back and was relieved that she wasn't hurt. The problem was, however, that they had no back way of getting into their property; it was solid rock up to a very steep bank. We had to get her through their house. It was a tiny house and we had to get her first into the kitchen, turn tightly into a sitting room and then out onto the street. She wouldn't go. We pushed, pulled, coaxed and got buckets of feed to try and entice her through, all to no avail.

We were still trying after 3 hours with a lot of people helping. Then some bright spark suggested we put blankets on the floors, to cover the tiles, as the sound of the hard tiles may have been frightening her. It worked. She walked straight into the kitchen, turned through a narrow door, through the sitting room and out into the street, greeted by a crowd of neighbours cheering and clapping. We quickly built a dividing wall so that it never happened again.

Huge ferias like the ones in Malaga are really spectacular. People dressed in colourful costumes, riding horses and dancing in the streets. The firework displays are breath-taking, the best I have ever seen.

About a week after we arrived, we gave a lift to a couple of young men who were walking up the mountain. One of them, Alex, had long blond hair down to his waist. They both came from Berlin. They were to be staying in the village for a few weeks. They came and visited us many times and brought lots of friends, it was very enjoyable for us all. Alex was very sweet and we became very fond of him. He had been separated from his mother by the Berlin wall and he was there when it was pulled down. He then ran for over 3 miles without stopping to see his mother; he hadn't seen her for some years.

Pamela to School

After the excitement of the arrival and the intoxication of the feria, we had to get down to the serious job of putting our youngest daughter Pamela, who was 11, into school. I went to see the local teacher and although I had been studying Spanish intensely for 2 years, with 2 private lessons a week, one with a qualified teacher and the other a 2-hour conversation with a Spanish friend in Taunton, I could barely understand half of what she was saying. Most Spanish people speak so fast and when you ask them to slow down, they say yes, of course, and continue as before. Pamela, at that point, could not understand anything, even though she also had been having lessons for 2 years, along with the rest of the family.

What I had to do was go to the British Consul in Malaga to establish at what level she should begin. She was then booked into the secondary school, which was in the next village. To get there, she walked with a group of children down a long goat track, over a dry river bed and then had a long very steep climb up the side of the hill over rocks. At times when it rained, the river was a raging torrent and they had to jump from rock to rock across the water. I watched her leave the house every day with that ragtag group of children to set off on her trek and wondered if I had taken leave of my senses. I had very serious doubts about the whole thing at that point, wondering what on earth we were doing there and wondering how I could possibly put her through this. She had left a quiet village in Somerset, where she was having flute, piano and riding lessons for this.

34

Dealing with the Language

Now she was struggling to understand the language and every night I had to sit for several hours with her translating all her lessons and books. We struggled together. First I would translate all the Spanish into English so that I could understand what it was that she was learning. Then, we had to write the homework and translate the whole lot back into Spanish. When I was stuck, I went to see the teacher and tried to grasp what she said. She talked at a gallop and I caught about one third of it. This went on for 6 months and then suddenly Pamela took off, left me behind totally, and was talking her head off fluently. I was hardly able to understand her when she was with her friends. She picked up the most unbelievable Andalucían mountain accent, which was pretty incomprehensible.

One day, sometime later, I was watching her do some geography homework and it was all very complicated. I asked her what it was all about. She knew what it was about, understood it and could answer the questions and discuss it at school but could not explain any of it to me in English. She understood it only in Spanish. I found this very unnerving. I then realised that if we weren't careful, she was going to forget her native tongue. We were the only people talking to her in English apart from our one English neighbour, whose wife had died just before we arrived there to live.

She had made a very close friendship with a young lad in the village more or less as soon as we arrived. He was a delightful, sensitive and very good-looking boy who worked hard and was intelligent. He seemed to be different from the other lads and I adored him. This friendship went on for 5 years. He spent a lot of time in our house and even though they were so young, they were both so crazy about each other, I sometimes wondered if they would end up getting married. The lad certainly thought so and was very deeply upset when Pamela eventually met someone else.

Back at home, we had all been learning Castellano, the traditional Spanish spoken in Madrid. My Spanish friend was from Leon in the north. Here in the village, it was as though they were speaking a different tongue altogether. A van used to arrive in the village every day and a man would get out and shout at the top of his voice, "Pekaaouw!" For the first month I was there, I

35

had no idea what he was saying. Initially, I was a bit shy about joining a whole group of women in front of a van selling stuff because they would all be talking their heads off and as soon as I began to speak, there would be complete silence and they would all be looking at me and listening intently. I finally realised that pekaaouw was pescado, the word for fish.

S is usually not pronounced in Andalucía and it takes some time to get used to it. The accents also vary tremendously from village to village. It seemed quite daunting. Listening to the news on television was the worst—or trying to watch a film. It seemed a lot more work was to be done. I had actually thought I spoke quite well until I got there. Some of my neighbours told me that I did speak well and it was them that didn't! Whatever it was, we still had to come to grips with all the different accents. What was a revelation to me was some time later when our Spanish friends from the stables visited us, they asked me if I had any idea that Pamela actually spoke like some wild mountain child. I had noticed that when she was around adults, I could more or less follow what she was saying, but when she was with her friends, I could hardly grasp a word.

There were words which were very similar to each other and great care had to be taken to say the right one. There were many examples. Pollo is chicken but polla is penis. Somebody I heard about decided she wanted a very tender female hen and asked the butcher in the supermarket for a large and tender polla. She wondered why the butchers behind the counter were in hysterics. After I had heard that tale, I would stand there and practise what to say before I dared open my mouth. One time before we moved there, I was visiting and I asked a car hire company if I had to put any olives in the engine—aceite is oil, aceituna is olive.

I found most people to be very kind and patient with the language. I walked into a police station one day and told the policeman in charge that I had just found a fine in my swearword and what was I supposed to do about it. Palabrisa is windscreen, palabrota is swearword. My daughter was with me and started trying to suppress a fit of laughter as we both realised what I had said. I also got the giggles. The policeman was very sweet.

My neighbour asked for a fire engine, bombero, instead of a gas bottle, bombona. I was showing a friend my kiln one day and got him to look in the spy hole in the door. I explained that when firing the kiln, the cones placed on the shelf fell over at certain temperatures. I said conos, with a tilde over the n, pronounced conyos, meaning genitals, instead of conos, meaning cones. He fell about laughing. The locals must have had such a laugh at our attempts to speak, but I knew that they did appreciate the efforts.

Will Arrives

One month after we arrived, there was a knock at the door and someone was calling out, "Hola!"

I went to the door and to my delight, there was our son Will. He had arrived as a surprise, hadn't told us and had arrived in Malaga on a feria day. Buses didn't seem to be running; he had had a job to get a taxi and Malaga was chaotic. It was great to see him. It had broken my heart to leave him behind. As we had driven away from him, I had an ache in my heart which was so strong, it was painful and it didn't leave my body for 48 hours. We all had a lot of fun together. He had already spent quite a bit of time there over the years before we moved there; he had gone over with friends and with his father. One time, with 3 friends, he had gone to a disco in the next village—a tiny disco with a few village people there. They all had very bright red faces from sunbathing, and the locals still remembered them many years later.

Lola

An amazing lady knocked on the door one day and presented her son to me and said he was the most fantastic decorator, very experienced and hard working. We were at the time in the middle of painting the place and needed a hand. She was such a bubbly happy person. I took him on. He turned out to be 15 and had never painted anything in his life. His mother and I became good friends. She was a widow with 7 children to feed, her husband had gone over the edge off a dirt track on his motorbike on his way home from the bar in a drunken state at the age of 39. They found him the next morning at the bottom of a gully. Many years later, she lost a son in the same way.

African Horse Disease

We could not have arrived in Spain at a worse time for our horse Tammy. They had the wretched peste equina, African horse disease. Thousands of horses were dying; I was very frightened when I heard about it. It was infectious and within 36 hours of contracting the disease, the animal would be dead. Horrendous stories of whole stables of beautiful Andalucían horses worth an absolute fortune dying abounded. They were not sure how the disease had arrived, there were many theories. An imported zebra from Africa was thought to be the cause. Imported meat was also blamed.

The government organised an emergency vaccination programme. Every horse in the country had to be vaccinated and marked with a large X branded on with a hot iron. Any horse not vaccinated or branded would be shot. Fortunately we were in a one horse town, ours being the only horse. There were however a few mules. We were all summoned to the top of the village in a square where the Ministry of Agriculture officials from Malaga were organising it and Tammy and the mules had their jabs and X, and Tammy coped with it much better than I did. I was very nervous about it. We were then provided with the paperwork to say she had had it done. Not everyone complied everywhere. We had someone bringing sheep from Granada on a regular basis for 3 months or so and his horse came with him, and I know that horse was not vaccinated. The government finally got it all under control but only after a great deal of heartbreak and loss.

An Unbearable Time

Several months after our arrival, our marriage collapsed and we parted, thinking that a temporary separation may help us. My husband returned to England. We had been in trouble for some time. It was a terrible and traumatic time. The pain and misery was unbearable. It was sad for all of us, and we hoped it would be only for a short while. We had had such a beautiful marriage. We were like a perfect couple, it was impossible to grasp that it had all gone wrong.

I found myself on the top of a mountain with 2 daughters to take care of, and I felt very frightened. I was in a foreign country, just about coping with the language and I had never had to pay a bill in my life. I had no idea how to pay for anything. We had no telephone; it took us 18 months to get it installed. I hardly knew where to begin.

Two of the 6 bedrooms were piled high with boxes and it took us several months to sort them out so that we could use the rooms. Outside in the upper side garden, we had the horse box full of pottery equipment, 2 kilns, 2 wheels and mountains more stuff. The lorry bringing our stuff from England had got to the bottom of the mountain and was so huge, the driver knew he would never get up to the village so had to call for a smaller lorry and transfer the stuff in batches. The kilns were so heavy, it was decided to put them in the horse box at the bottom of the mountain before bringing them up and we could store them in the box for the time being.

A few weeks later after Jack left, he returned and built us a stable for the horse and also put up a room to the side to house my pottery kiln. He also made a lovely patio out of stone slabs to the side. It was a tremendous relief to have somewhere to put the horse at night and when it was raining or very hot. We had been using a small abandoned house down the road; we were given permission to do so. It had been used for goats and was eventually turned into a pleasant house. It was perfect for her, it had a window and door. The only problem was that children went in there at night and got on her back. We were pretty cross when we found out.

Jack and I still did not seem to be able to communicate with each other very well, however, and after a few weeks, he returned again to the U.K.

Not long after being on our own came the first warning that we had trouble looming ahead. An old boy I was chatting to told me I was going to have trouble with my land and that the mayor would be after me.

"What!" I said. "You have to be joking! The land is mine; I have bought it and have the Escritura to prove it."

"You are going to have trouble," he said, "the mayor says the land is his."

I thought he had it wrong, but I felt very uneasy.

Sandra Working

Sandra found work training horses in some stables a few miles away. We had found out about the stables when one day in our local bar, we were having a drink and a chat and 12 horses arrived in the village. Their riders tied them all up in the churchyard. They crowded into the tiny bar there, 11 men and 1 woman, all talking their heads off. I couldn't catch much of it. After about 10 minutes, the lady turned to me and asked me if I was English. It was wonderful to meet another English lady and I was very impressed that she had ridden for many kilometres up from the coast across country with 11 Spanish guys. I thought she was very brave. They looked like a pretty wild bunch to me. She assured me they were her friends and told me where all the horses had come from.

We went visiting and found the owners, Manuel and Pepe, very pleasant. We became friends. There was a bar on the premises, and we enjoyed time there eating and drinking and meeting people. Sandra started work there, helping to train their unruly thoroughbreds. We had some difficulty trying to accept their way of doing things. They had 65 horses stabled and no land whatsoever, apart from the yard in front of the stables and an arena. Most of the horses were owned by various people living in Malaga, and some came out at weekends to see them. Sometimes they didn't come out for months. A lot of the people didn't pay their stable bills either, and it was pretty hard for Manuel and Pepe, who had to feed the animals and maintain them. Some of those horses didn't leave their stables for 3 months at a time. Their stables were very small, but they were all well fed and had clean bedding every day. The owners were meant to come and exercise them regularly but most of them didn't bother. The horses were just a status symbol, something to tell their friends about.

There were quite a few English stables along the coast and they thoroughly disapproved of the way Spanish stables and their horses were managed. We found the tack they used quite awful. Sandra and I would be looking round for the best tack when we saddled up at the stables and could only find old, rusty and quite horrible huge bits that went in the horse's mouth. On one occasion, a horse I was riding spent the whole time frothing at the mouth because the bit was so uncomfortable, poor thing.

Nose bands were made of rusty serrated metal which dug into their faces and made cuts and wounds. They were appalling. We did discuss these things with Miguel and Pepe, and they found they had one set of English tack, but on the whole it was all so different to what we had been used to.

Sandra began exercising and training their horses. She had spent years training our own horse, show jumping, cross country and dressage, competing and winning 59 rosettes. Those horses were very big and strong and after being stabled for so long without exercise were a real handful. One day, a horse who was just raring to go, managed to buck her off and then tread on her ribs. She was rushed to hospital in a great deal of pain. She was examined and x-rayed and told there was nothing wrong. They brought her home. She lay on the sofa for days, hardly being able to move for the pain. It wasn't until a year later when she went back to England for a holiday and had a further x-ray that she was told she had 3 broken ribs. The hospital had x-rayed the wrong part of her ribs. The owners of the stables were very kind. They came to visit her and brought piles of presents and flowers. It took her some time to recover.

When Manuel from the stables heard Pamela speak, he was simply incredulous. He asked me if I had any idea how badly she spoke and that she was actually talking like some wild mountain goat child with a very strong accent! I had long since noticed that although I could understand her when she was around adults, I could hardly grasp a word of what she said when she was with her friends. She had certainly picked up the local dialect.

As a result of Sandra working at the stables, we were all able to ride whenever we wanted. We had some amazing rides. We rode for miles, and on one occasion it had rained heavily and the river nearby was running with water. We and the horses had a great time splashing in the river through the water and then clattering up into tiny villages and parading through the narrow streets. It was exhilarating.

I went out for several hours one day with a group of men from the stables. We went to the beach and rode for miles there. Most of the horses wouldn't go near the sea and shied away. We went through rivers, up into the hills, through villages and over more hills—it was stunning. It was very hot and at times they really pushed the horses too hard. We also had 2 big dogs with us trying to keep up. I felt sorry for all the animals. It all seemed far too strenuous in such hot weather, and they were all worn out when we got back. A great time, however, was had by all of us.

The stables put on some very interesting events. One party was hoping to serve about 200 people with paella. Lots of riders dressed in traditional clothes pranced about on magnificent horses. Manuel rode a huge black stallion. They didn't castrate their horses because they wanted them fiery and full of energy. The paella pan was about 2 metres in diameter—enormous. Only 50 people arrived on that occasion, so there was a great deal of paella to eat.

Some Wonderful Visitors

A few months after meeting our German friend Alex, he and 3 of his friends arrived unexpectedly late one night in a camper van. They were on their way to Morocco. We were happy to see them, but Sandra was quite alarmed by his friends as they looked like quite a motley bunch. She was not happy about them staying in the house, and we squabbled about it. I felt that if Alex was such a nice guy, then his friends must also be, despite their appearance. She would only allow Alex to stay in the house the first night, and the other 3 slept in the churchyard in sleeping bags. I felt most uneasy about that.

Next day, they spent their time with us and we got to know Alex's friends. One of them was doing handstands up and down the hill outside our house, with a crowd of villagers watching him. Joe seemed sweet—and then there was Thierry. He was the one who had made Sandra nervous. He was French, very swarthy, very scruffy, but extremely good-looking. It looked as though he hadn't washed for a couple of months. He was also most charming. Our English neighbour invited them all in and gave them drinks and we had a very pleasant evening together. He also offered to mend a bed for them in their camper van. It was all taken to pieces in the road outside our house and repaired.

By the end of the day, Sandra felt easier about having them all in the house and we had plenty of bedrooms for them to sleep in. We managed to rustle up food for them all. They then all left to go to Morocco. After a month or so, they called in again on the way back. It was very exciting, as they parked their camper van outside and emptied its contents onto the road. They had piles of rugs, beautiful cloth and robes with hoods like a monk's habit, which they all put on to show us. They paraded up and down the road showing off their wares, and we all took lots of photographs. They certainly kept the village entertained. Then out came crates of dates and piles of fruit and nuts and they were also laid out in the road. They stayed again for a couple of weeks and we really enjoyed their company. They made us beautiful drinks in the juicer from dates and milk, nuts, fruits and honey.

With 4 strong men staying in the house, I decided to ask them to help me get my kilns out of the horse box parked outside and down into the house. The largest kiln was extremely heavy and it took all 4 of them 3½ hours to get the kiln out and down a slope, with the use of wooden planks to help. I had no idea where to put it once I got it out, but fearing it would get ruined outside with nowhere under cover to keep it, we moved it into the kitchen.

Thierry was stunning. One evening again in our English neighbour's house, he found something amusing and fell on the carpet, rolling around in hysterics. He behaved in a very uninhibited way and seemed to be always laughing. I noticed that Sandra was becoming entranced. At the end of their stay when they were all due to leave and return to Germany, Thierry did not want to go with them. He remained behind and they all went off and left him. Now I began to worry. Sandra was 17. I wondered how long he would stay and how on earth he would get home to France.

After a couple of weeks, Thierry and Sandra said they wanted to go to Sevilla together. I told them they had to be joking, there was no chance whatsoever. They kept on at me, begging and pleading. I told them there was no way they were going. They kept on all day for two or three days. I said we hardly know the man, and Sandra said he was a friend of Alex, an argument which now suited her. I might have liked him, but going off with him to Sevilla was another matter, she was not going. We were all beginning to lose our rag. Arguments were going on all the time, it was wearing me down. Thierry told me that he had an English friend in Sevilla called Judith, he had rung her and they could stay with her. I didn't believe him. They both insisted it was true, and they would be perfectly safe staying with her. He promised to take perfect care of her. It was like trying to stop a train. I caved in. I wished her father was there, I felt like I wasn't coping.

I got some money for her and drove them both to Malaga to the bus station. As I left them, I turned round and looked at them; they were sitting on a bench. They were both absolutely stunning. Sandra was beautiful, dressed in tartan trousers covered in safety pins, black boots covered in studs, a black leather jacket which was half threadbare and covered in zips, and her blond hair was long and utterly wild. He was dark skinned; a huge mop of very black hair stood on end and was quite gorgeous. They looked amazing together. I felt very frightened. When I told my neighbours, they thought I had taken leave of my senses.

Sandra rang and told me Sevilla was fabulous, full of churches and beautiful streets and buildings. She said they were both fine. I fretted the whole time. They stayed a week and returned home safely, much to my great relief. Thierry stayed with us for another week or so and then we put him on a train back to France. I then heard what really happened. Judith didn't exist, as I had strongly suspected. They had arrived in Sevilla and Thierry had known of a huge abandoned mansion in the middle of the city somewhere and they had climbed up to the top floor where the roof had caved in and had slept under the stars. They had lit fires and cooked food there. The police had seen the fire and arrived to investigate. Sandra was terrified. They managed to talk their way out of it. Life out in the world could be quite scary. Thierry had tried to persuade her to go to Morocco, she fortunately declined.

Unfortunately, a few weeks later when my husband arrived to visit, he walked in the house, saw the kiln in the kitchen and told me only I could put a kiln in the kitchen. I tried to explain my reasons but burst into tears, and he walked out and drove off. It was pretty obvious we weren't getting on. I went out into the street and cried on a neighbour's shoulder. I really had hoped we might get back together. We were all terribly upset that he had just walked out and left us as soon as he had arrived, but he did come back the next day. During that stay, he suggested we got a few blokes together and brought the kiln outside and into the small building he had put up especially for the purpose. Six men and some planks moved it easily and it was a great relief that I could hopefully start to use it.

Looking for Work and Friends

A few months after we arrived, I felt I had to start getting my own work together. In England, I had had a centre in Somerset for healing and food allergy testing and before I left, I had all my literature translated into Spanish by my teacher. At that moment in time, I could not imagine how I would really get started. I found that the people were very open to healings and I had been treating people in the village and other villages nearby right from when we bought the house. It started when I offered treatment to some dear friends and the word spread. Wherever I went, I was asked to help someone. I didn't charge anybody and was given wine, raisins, lemons and oranges as payment.

Then I read in the coastal English paper about a healing centre in Fuengirola, and the article said that a qualified NFSH healer had just arrived on the coast. Oh, I thought, I must ring them and tell them about me also. When I rang, I discovered it was me that they were talking about. I arranged to go and meet them and was very warmly welcomed. I was introduced to everyone and gave a talk about my work at some big outdoor function. From that moment, I began to go twice a week to help run the centre and help train healers. It was a huge relief to be working again. They were a mixed group of people from many different countries, and I made lots of new friends.

The first evening there, I was invited to stay overnight with an English guy and his Swedish girlfriend. They lived in a beautiful villa with a couple of boxer dogs and two horses. They had quite a stormy relationship and parted for a while. They eventually decided to move to Malta and take all their animals with them. The last time I saw Lena, their horses were in Barcelona, getting ready to be shipped over. They had not been there long when Colin died of a heart attack, and despite many attempts at contacting Lena, none of us ever heard from her again. I was worried as she had told a friend that if it all went wrong, she would commit suicide and take her animals with her.

A delightful Danish couple approached me when I initially joined the group, and we became very close friends. They were both homeopaths. I spent a lot of time with them and had a lot of fun. They had a lovely villa with a pool near the castle in Fuengirola. After some years, their marriage ended and he went to live with a much younger lady from Sevilla, a nurse who he had been treating. He was 65 when they had a child together.

An Invitation

A Belgian guy training to be a therapist in our group appeared to be delightful, charming and friendly. I had known him for some months when he invited me and the two girls to go and live with him and take our animals with us. This was quite an astonishing offer and although I could not imagine any possibility of this occurring, it sounded like a way of ending the excruciating loneliness I was feeling at the collapse of my marriage. Pamela and I, however, did accept an invitation to go for a weekend. He had a great house in the mountains with a lot of land and horses. The Saturday began rather strangely with a woman arriving unexpectedly to stay. She informed me that she was a stripper and an old friend of our host.

Later that evening, we all went out into their local town to some club, although Pamela was rather young. But I couldn't leave her alone. Next morning, the friend took her to visit some English friends in a village who had fallen on hard times. They were living in a hovel furnished from the rubbish tip, with barely a thing to eat. My daughter was very dismayed.

Later that day, our friend took Pamela riding on a couple of huge horses and despite my pleas to take care of her and only walk slowly; he immediately set the horses to gallop as madly as possible through the woods. Pamela was very scared, and I wasn't at all pleased, to say the least, especially as when they returned, he rode deliberately into our boxer dog and made him squeal in pain. This was because earlier, our boxer had had a scuffle with one of his dogs, and he had picked Saul up and thrown him from some height onto his back. We almost walked out at that moment.

We soon began to realise that he was very cruel to animals. All his dogs and cats were almost starving. All he gave them to eat was a little cooked white rice. If one of his dogs did anything wrong, he hung it on a tree. We learned later that one couple we knew had trusted him to take care of their dog and cat when they moved abroad and were horrified to learn that he had just left them to die and had even found it amusing to do so. After some lunch on Sunday, we were relieved that the weekend had come to an end, and we gratefully made our escape.

Renting Rooms

We were approached by a local language academy where students learned Spanish. The owner lived abroad and organised groups of people, mostly youngsters and Germans, to spend 3 weeks or more in the village. He could bring more over if he had more rooms; I agreed readily, we had 3 spare bedrooms. We had a lot of sorting out of boxes to do and the academy loaned us some beds, we got a bit of extra furniture and then we were in business. It turned out to be great fun and it was good for my daughters, as we regularly had a houseful of interesting young people of both sexes. The food was served in the academy.

I was also delighted to be offered a job teaching yoga there, as I am a trained yoga teacher. I was given a beautiful cool room in the garden surrounded by beautiful plants, and it was great fun teaching yoga again, even though there were a few problems with the languages. I remember one student who spoke German, Turkish and Russian. I spoke English, Spanish and French! Six languages between us and we couldn't communicate! I had done A level German but had forgotten so much of it. The only way we were able to communicate was by my demonstrating the yoga postures and for the meditations, someone had to translate. I was also asked to teach pottery there. But it was rather difficult as I hadn't got any of my equipment organised at that stage.

We had quite a lot of fun people staying. They came because they knew it was a village in the mountains and this was what they wanted, so generally they were prepared. We would have as many as 36 students staying in the village in the summer and they certainly brought a lot of colour and interest. The locals would get a lot more work, there was cleaning to be done, lots of cooking, driving and so on. Cookery classes were available to learn lots of the local dishes and I was pleased to go along. Teachers were brought in from outside and there was a lot of gossiping going on about what the locals thought of the students and what they thought of the locals. I heard about some quite scandalous gossip that they were learning about the private lives of some of the villagers, all part of the curriculum!

47

However, there were some people who were utterly aghast at the location, the road up the mountain to get there and the lack of things to do in the village. They had not realised it was so very rural. Some were so shocked that they left immediately. Most of those staying with us were fine, but we had our share of problems. One couldn't cope with our boxer dog, she was terrified of him and after one night, she left. Three young girls of about 18 were woken up at 4 a.m. every morning by next door's cockerel so one night, they got up at 3.30 a.m. and tried to throw a bucket of water over the poor thing. They couldn't see what they were doing in the dark and the cockerel kept crowing. They left the next morning. Others were kept awake by the howling dogs which roamed the streets. A couple of girls complained about the cats we had.

One saucy girl moved herself and all her luggage into a better bedroom whilst we were out. I had just prepared it for my son, who was arriving the next day. She was most put out when I asked her to move back again. She thought our house was at the disposal of the academy and they could do as they pleased. She had arrived at the village on an 850cc Honda motorbike dressed in black leather and had caused quite a sensation. Most of the young men in the village had 50cc mopeds and screamed about the village like a swarm of angry bees.

One young man of about 30 from Berlin actually sat me down and said he wanted to have a talk with me. He said I had obviously lost the plot, living in such a hellhole and what on earth did I think I was doing there? He said I just was not the type of person who should live in such an isolated place and how could I have been so cruel to force my daughters to live there? He couldn't live there under any circumstances, and it was beyond his comprehension. I tried as nicely as I could to explain that this was what we wanted and we were happy there, but he got very angry and kept insisting it wasn't right. In the end, I had to get cross with him and tell him firmly to stop going on. Next day, he apologised. I guess it was pretty different from Berlin.

There were lots of activities arranged for them and we were invited to paellas and parties. I was paid to drive a group of them to Granada one day, travelling the scenic route and enjoying ourselves on the way. We stopped at a spa and just outside, we were encouraged to get into a tiny tub of hot water alongside some rocks which we had to clamber over. About 5 of us managed to squash into the tub at a time with great hilarity, after which we wandered, paddling in the river and having a picnic.

Sevillana dance classes were started in the village for the students, and Pamela and I joined up. It was far more difficult than I had imagined. There were several parts that made up the whole with a precise order of steps. We managed to grasp it all for the first 3 lessons and then it got difficult. We were having to write it all out to try and learn it. There was no way either of us was going to be a natural, even though I am crazy about dancing. Spanish children learn at a very early age and are so graceful. The adults danced in such an elegant way, the men so arrogant, so haughty and so sexy, I never tired of watching them. At ferias, everybody seemed to know how to do it without effort. I was dragged up to dance a few times and made my best stab at it, even though I couldn't get it right. It was a lot of fun.

Some Interesting Neighbours

It was most fortunate around this time that a wonderful Italian lady who had a house in the village and lived in Madrid decided to move to the village permanently with her husband. She and I became very close friends and had wonderful times together. We managed to borrow a lot of unusual films on video coming out of the States and we all spent many evenings together. We also had days out shopping, having parties, going to clubs and so on. She was an incredible support to us all. Her husband was a writer and journalist and did a lot of travelling.

There were many eccentric and interesting characters in the village. There were two gentlemen living together, Carlo was a weaver and made beautiful handmade articles such as bags, pouches and covers. Michel was a French harpsichordist. They lived in quite a large house. Michel was well known and travelled Europe giving concerts. He owned several harpsichords and gave magnificent concerts in our village church. A friend of mine who was staying at the time attended one and said it was the most beautiful concert she had ever heard. With the very high ceilings, the acoustics had a haunting and magical effect.

Carlo met a German lady who was some kind of therapist and they moved to France, had 3 children together and set up a business of growing tomatoes. With Michel away doing concerts most of the time, the house in the village started to fall into disrepair. Carlo came back one day and employed a young village girl of 14 to be their nanny and took her back to Germany to live. It seems that Carlo then began sleeping with this girl and she became pregnant. The marriage fell apart and the girl was sent to Malaga to live with her grandmother. The last I heard, Carlo was suffering from severe depression.

Right opposite Michel and Carlo's house was a small cottage owned by a German family who used it for holidays. On the side was a tiny log shed and into this log shed, every winter, moved a very eccentric gentleman, somewhere in his sixties, with long grey hair down his back and a very long beard. He put a blanket on the floor amongst the piles of wood and that was where he lived for 6 months. He was sweet and gentle and very hard of hearing. He took to visiting us frequently and he was intensely passionate about weeds. He would arrive on my doorstep with a bunch of wild plants which I could barely recognise and tell me how to make soup with them. He had a piece of land out in the wilds where he insisted on growing every type of weed imaginable. One day in my garden, I bent down to pull out a weed growing on the step and he screamed. He told me that every weed is actually a plant. I have never felt the same about 'weeds' from that moment on.

One winter, he forced a connecting door from the log shed and got into the cottage and used the family's facilities. When the family next arrived, they were naturally pretty upset and threw him out. He then moved into Carlo's house across the street, which by this time was in serious disrepair. The roof was leaking badly all over and he could only put his blanket on one bit of the floor. He managed to make a fire in the grate and cook up his wild plant concoctions. I visited him sometimes, the patio was a mass of plants and it amazed me how someone could live like that, but he seemed very happy. It seemed he had successfully avoided all authorities in Germany for many years and was therefore not receiving any assistance whatsoever.

Some Unexpected Proposals

Early one spring he came to say goodbye. He was returning to Germany, where he lived in the upper part of somebody's barn, donkeys lived below. We said our farewells and I said I looked forward to seeing him again in the autumn. He was leaving that afternoon. The following morning, I found a note through my door from him, saying that he hadn't gone because he had fallen in love with me and didn't want to leave. He asked me to write and tell him how I felt about him and what he should do. I was so utterly stunned, I found myself not knowing what on earth to say to him.

I had no romantic notions towards him whatsoever, he was just a friend and although I love eccentrics, he was a bit too eccentric for me to consider him as a partner. He was completely penniless and I had a house to run and a family to take care of. I wasn't prepared to take him in. I did not want to hurt him so I didn't answer his letter. Afterwards, I realised that I should have gone and talked to him, and I felt bad about that. He left a few days later. We did, somehow, seem to attract every eccentric within a several mile radius of our home.

One day in the square stood a nice-looking blond guy, his very blond child and a beautiful donkey, and I stopped and spoke to them for at the most 5 minutes, as they looked sweet together. A few days later, he came over the mountains from some remote village and roared up to our front door on his motorbike, accompanied by a wild-looking man with a big mop of black curly hair and a long black beard, on his own bike. I was out working and the girls answered the front door. Every few days, the same thing happened and it was only about their eleventh visit that they found me in. In the meantime, some neighbours informed me that the dark hairy guy was a known thief and had in fact robbed them of a motorbike a couple of years before. Another 3 neighbours had asked me if one of these characters was in fact my boyfriend, they had called so often.

So when they eventually found me in, I went flying out. "What on earth do you both want and why do you keep banging on my door and scaring the hell out of my daughters?"

The blond guy said, "We got on so well in the square when we met that I thought we could get to know each other."

"Good heavens!" I said. "All I did was stroke your donkey and say how sweet it was! Can you both please go away and leave us all alone!" A shame really, as the blond guy seemed quite nice and was evidently divorced, I had learned, but as his friend was a thief, it blew his respectability somewhat.

In the meantime, we were getting on with our lives. I was in constant emotional pain about the breakdown of my marriage. It was like an illness, it never went away and no matter what I did; I was hurting badly. I couldn't really believe it, it felt like a nightmare. We had been so happy for so long. Things hadn't worked out the way we had planned, and it was not going to be easy to try and mend things with so much distance between us. We seemed to have reached the point where we could not communicate properly. We had no telephone and could only rely on messages via our English neighbour, who kindly allowed us to use his or use a public phone when we went out to the coast.

Renting Rooms to the Public

We had also started renting out rooms to the general public. Various people arrived in the village looking for rooms, and the local taverna sent them down to me. We had quite a variety of people. A delightful poet from Madrid came with the intention of staying for a few months, but it seems I quoted him too much money for the room; I was very disappointed to lose him, as he was very sweet and gentle. The owner of the bar advised me how much to charge, and I took his advice. An Englishman came and stayed for several weeks, trying to set up a business. I was able to earn extra money by translating for him, typing and telephoning. Unfortunately, his mobile phone didn't work in the village and every time he needed to use it, he had to drive a couple of miles out of the village and up the hill.

A rough-looking guy arrived one day with a girl and parked his car with the front in a bush up against a bank. He asked me if I could lend the girl some evening clothes to go to a casino. They had no luggage. I was pretty dubious and cautiously offered to lend her a good dress but suggested he put down some money to cover it. He took offence and told me not to bother. The next day, someone asked me if I had seen the front of his car which was smashed up. It was practically non-existent and had no lights. I was getting nervous. They stayed about 3 nights, and I felt too jumpy about them and I made some excuse about the room being booked. He knew I wanted to get rid of them and became quite nasty. They went upstairs to pack and smashed several bottles of wine all around the room. The entire floor was covered in broken glass, including all under the bed.

When he left, he got out the biggest bundle of money I had ever seen, peeled some notes off to pay me and then informed me that he had a method of winning in casinos, but as soon as the casino owners realised, they would throw him out and he then had to move on to the next one. He told me he made a fortune. He told me off for wanting him out and was very aggressive. He also gave me advice on how to organise the house in a different way in order to have a separate entrance for people renting. I tried to be as pleasant as possible whilst willing him to leave. I was relieved to see the back of them. He had obviously picked the girl up on the way.

Going Well

Pamela was getting on very well with school and had made loads of friends. She was treated and accepted as one of the village children and was in and out of everybody's houses in our village and other villages. They all loved to go to a nearby village discotheque, and I used to drive loads of kids there. It was amazing how many kids I could pack into my Seat Panda. It had a soft top and they loved to stand up and put their heads out of the roof.

All kinds of work was materialising for me. I had started giving English lessons to one of the children, then a few more started with a couple of adults. I went into Malaga and bought myself some good books. Word had got about that I was a healer and people were coming for healings. We had had locks put in our bedroom doors by this stage as a safety measure for when we rented rooms.

Sandra wasn't finding it so easy to make friends, and she had nobody to go out with. I felt sorry for her. She was only 17 so I offered to go clubbing with her and that really started something. I had been a frustrated dancer. I learned Scottish and ballroom dancing at school. Then, when I left school, I enrolled in further classes. I got to dance quite a bit when I worked for Mitsubishi in London because they had a club in Chelsea and were always putting on social events, so I got to do a lot of waltzes and foxtrots.

We had lived in Nassau for a year and went to all the clubs there, boogying away the nights. Jack was happy to dance there because blues and reggae were our kind of music. I recall a wedding we were invited to, where we were embarrassingly put at the head of the table and treated as very special guests just because we were white. I danced with every man in the room that night; I counted them up afterwards—28 men. My husband enjoyed himself watching, and I was utterly exhausted but utterly exhilarated. However, back in Somerset, I could never get my husband on his feet on any occasion—weddings, local hops, parties, nothing. I dragged him to ballroom dance classes, but all we did was fall over each other's feet so we gave up after a few sessions.

Now I had the chance to make up for all the dancing I had never got to do. I went a bit wild. I think my own mid-life crisis must have been kicking in. Sandra was even wilder. She had a crazy thing going on where she planted her feet firmly on the floor and shook her head violently, her mop of blond hair flying about. She shook her body wildly, all in bare feet and mini skirt and she would cause quite a sensation. Everybody around her would stop and stare, especially the men. Some of the girls got quite jealous and one night some girl picked her shoes up and threw them over a wall down into some deserted dark area full of rubbish about 12 feet below. We had to get a security officer to go and collect them.

It seemed a shame she had to go with her mum, but I was only 8 stone 5lbs and was very young at heart. We got on very well and enjoyed going to a whole variety of different clubs all along the coast and up in the hills. The clubs there were sensational. A new club on the coast by the sea opened while we were there. It had various dance floors on different levels, and lots of different bars, all open-air but with a small closed area for when it was cold or raining. They were mostly full of youngsters, but I was relieved to see older men and women, including some mothers I knew from surrounding villages so I didn't feel too out of place. They didn't open until about midnight and sometimes even later than that. It was so much cooler at that time, and then they stayed open until about 8am.

The most astonishing club was one in Torremolinos. It had been converted from an underground car park. It was divided into various sections and from the ceilings hung all sorts of crazy things—a motor car, an aeroplane, a motorbike. One of the circular dance floors rose up whilst you were dancing on it to about 6 feet off the floor. We often started off in one or two bars, then went from one club to another, arriving home at about 6am. Pamela stayed with a neighbour but as she got older, if we were going somewhere suitable, we took her with us. It was harmless fun, and I kept a very close eye on my daughters. Sometimes we would go with friends in the village or with the students who were staying with us.

There were various problems going back home up the mountain afterwards. Sometimes there was a fog so thick, we couldn't see more than 2 metres in front of us, and with dangerous drops over the edge, it was pretty scary. One morning, I thought what was all that furniture everywhere? I had driven into the rubbish tip by mistake, the fog was so thick. It was difficult to get out. On another occasion, we were tanking up the hill, not expecting to see anyone coming down at 5.30 a.m. We went round a bend to be confronted with a rubbish truck which had just been up and unloaded its pile. He was going fast, couldn't stop, put his hand on his horn and nearly sent us into the next world. He must have missed us by a hair's breadth. I was badly shaken up. It was a bit embarrassing arriving home as other people were getting up. I recall one Sunday morning, we got in at 7 a.m. and our neighbour was up a ladder, already painting his house.

Nightmares Ahead

The first I knew I had serious problems was one Sunday morning. Wondering what all the noise was, I went outside to find 9 people and an assistant from the town hall in my garden.

"Excuse me, but what are you all doing here?" I asked.

The assistant informed me that he was showing the people various plots of land for sale in order to build a house and this piece of land was one of them. I went a bit crazy. I started shouting and rushed indoors to get my Escritura, waving it in their faces and telling them in no uncertain terms that the land was mine and they could kindly remove themselves at once.

The assistant tried arguing but I was having none of it. The prospective purchasers all looked very embarrassed. They all left and 20 minutes later, the mayor arrived He walked deliberately into my garden and stood there defiantly. I asked him what he was doing there. He informed me very clearly and firmly that the land was his, and he was selling it to have a house built. I started yelling at him. I told him I had bought the land, had all the necessary legal documents and that under no circumstances was it his. He started walking towards me in the street and I was walking backwards.

He said, "Don't you shout at me in public!"

I screamed at him as loud as I possibly could and said, "I shall shout at you as much as I like! Don't you think you can come down here trying to steal my land, because you won't get away with it!"

By this time, he had me pinned with my back against my neighbour's car, and he put his face a couple of inches from mine and said, "THIS VILLAGE IS OURS!"

Little did he know that that comment would be printed in almost every Spanish national newspaper at a later date. What he meant by that was he was the mayor and had been then for more than 20 years. He had 7 brothers and sisters in the village with all their families, and he thought the village belonged to him and his family. His father had been mayor before him. He and his family had got away with dominating the village and its people so totally that everybody other than family was scared of him. He had a great deal of power. My neighbour was his sister and we were good friends and on this occasion, she defended me vigorously. She told him to leave me alone and go home, that I had bought the house and land many years before. At that point in time, we had owned the property for about 7 or 8 years.

This was the beginning of a very long battle that lasted for several years, not just for me but for many other families who had been downtrodden and had lost their homes thanks to this man and his assistant. The battle took off with great strength at a later date with the arrival of an unexpected ally.

In the Meantime

Sandra was by this time working as a nanny in Marbella. She was in some fabulous villa with a pool near the beach and quite enjoying it. They had 3 children and two yachts, and she was seeing a different world from inland Spain. We visited her and she came home regularly. The woman who employed her was an actress and her husband said he was building property. They were a very dysfunctional family with a lot of scandal

56

surrounding them. The woman, it seemed, was a lesbian and had a much older lover, and the husband obviously wasn't coping very well with the situation. There were times when he wanted Sandra and the children to go out with him on one of his yachts, but she would have none of it. She didn't want to find herself in a difficult situation in the middle of the sea. I wasn't sure who was the most danger to my daughter, the mother or the father. Sandra came across some quite embarrassing scenes at times. Nevertheless, it was very interesting for her.

Some Wonderful Friends

We became very good friends with a lovely family in the village. They lived in Malaga and came out to a house they had in the village at weekends. I met their son Jose. He was quite ill and had recently broken up with his Danish wife and returned from Denmark, where he had been living. He was emotionally wrecked about it and was also badly missing her children. He invited me to go and help him wash his car in the river! It was such a rare sight to see water in the river. It was fun to park it right in the middle of the water and an easy way to get it clean, though not very environmentally friendly. It gave us a chance to get away from the village and have a good talk about ourselves and our situations.

We went out together on and off for years, and it helped me a lot. It was wonderful to have a friend and someone to have meals with and go dancing with. He took me to all sorts of restaurants and bars I would never have known about in the back streets of Malaga and along the coast. He helped me out with problems and was good to my daughters. He would take us all out sometimes; he took us to the summer fair in Malaga and also to the Easter parade through the streets. Sometimes a friend of his would join us or a friend of mine who was staying on holiday with us would. We had a lot of fun. Sometimes we would just sit at night on the beach and it was beautiful.

His family owned a very large piece of land, a huerta, full of vegetables and fruit trees. It had a little house on it. I was extremely fond of his father Enrique. He kindly invited us to put Tammy in there to eat the grass, which was a godsend as I needed grazing for her. It was safe as they kept an eye on her for me. He gave us bags of lemons, oranges and fruits and vegetables of all kinds. He even planted a whole area with oats especially for Tammy. I supplied him with sacks of horse manure. We tethered her in his land on long ropes, but she still managed to break free quite regularly and eat some of his runner beans, some of his roses and generally cause havoc as animals do. She was crazy about runner bean plants and one day, poor Enrique was knocked down a ditch in her rush to get at them. She had to go through a tiny door to get into the huerta and managed to rip it right off its hinges one day in her rush to get in there. She loved it so much because there was so much to eat. Enrique loved having her and they got on really well. He also took care of her when I went away and would bring her back and put her in her stable at night.

He had the most amazing knowledge of plants and healing the body naturally and would take me for walks over the hills and try to teach me which plant was which. There were so many different herbs there, lots I had never heard of. I struggled to keep up with the names of them all and he would explain their uses. He had a nephew running a health food shop in Malaga, and he himself worked there sometimes to help out. He loaned me books on these herbs and their medicinal properties.

After being hospitalised following a heart attack, he embarked on a programme of eating lemons in order to heal his heart. He was utterly convinced that fresh lemons could not only cut cholesterol but heal the body of many ailments. He ate about 3 or 4 lemons a day for several weeks and when he went for his check up, it was discovered that his heart was completely healthy. This made a strong impression on me, and I am now never out of fresh lemons. I usually have half a dozen in the fridge at any time. However, his heart attack may been brought on by the constant fights he had with his wife Maria. They never stopped arguing and shouting at each other, calling each other the most dreadful things, and generally swearing at and insulting each other.

Will It Ever Rain?

There are a great deal of problems with water, or the lack of it, in southern Spain. Whilst we lived there, we had a period of 5 years with no rain whatsoever. It was utterly traumatic for the countryside, trees, animals and humans. Everybody ran out of water and our village had to buy water in. It came in from France in a huge tanker. Millions of trees died. Hans, a friend who lived in the back of beyond with about 4 acres of land, lost 108 trees of almond, olive and carob. He was naturally very upset about it and then had the problem of dealing with all those dead trees.

Our source of mountain water dried up, which made it very difficult for the passing herds of goats which came through grazing as they always stopped to refresh themselves, not to mention every other animal and bird. I left out bowls of water every day for whatever animal may need it. We were well advised right from the beginning to put a water tank on the top of our roof, which was a godsend. Only a few other houses had them. When everybody else had run out of water supplied by the village, we had at least 2 more days supply. Using it sparingly, it sometimes lasted a further 3 days. I used to keep buckets and containers filled in case of emergency. After all, we had a horse, a dog and lots of cats too to think of, as well as ourselves. It was very frightening to run out of water.

It seemed a miracle to me that anything at all survived in such a bleak and barren landscape. The hills were utterly parched, brown and shrivelled. It was like a desert in places, dry and dusty, with the sun beating down relentlessly. I was getting worried about the lack of hay available for Tammy, as grass wasn't growing anywhere. The hay all came down from the north and there was a shortage. I regularly went searching in remote areas of the river beds between various villages and found succulent plants such as wild sweet peas and different grasses were still growing in places where it was shaded from the sun and had some underground water. I had a four wheel drive by this time and was able to get it across very stony river beds. I picked piles of suitable food for her and loaded up the vehicle. I saw to it that she never went short of fresh nourishing food.

People everywhere were praying for rain and I joined them. I heard about groups who were practising African rain dances! It was so desperately needed. The day it rained was such an utter joy. I went out into my garden and just stood there and looked up to heaven and thanked God. It was pure ecstasy to just stand in it and get utterly soaked to the skin with the beautiful liquid pouring out of the sky. I thought of us all, of every animal, every plant, every tree and flower and every bird and I was so thankful.

How many wild animals and birds must have died during that time!

We were visiting Hans one time. He was the German boyfriend of a very close Danish friend of mine. They had romantically met each other in my house when I was running an art and pottery weekend course. In order to get to his farm, which was vaguely near Colmenar, north of Malaga, we had to be met at a restaurant and then follow him downhill for 8 miles on dirt tracks. This time, we had our uncle Fred with us, who was over on holiday from Vancouver Island in Canada. Standing on Hans' patio overlooking his land, my uncle asked where the boundary was of Hans' land. I pointed down and told him, "There, by that river."

"What river?" he asked.

I replied, "There, just there, can't you see the river?"

"No, I can't," he said, "I can't see a river anywhere."

I looked at him and thought what was the matter with him, it was perfectly clear. Then I realised of course that it was a dry river bed I was pointing to, as they all were, and explained this to him.

"Oh my, what a crazy country this is," he said, "no water in the rivers! Whoever heard of a river with no water!"

Before I moved to Spain, I used to complain, as all English people do, about the rain, but after those experiences I have changed completely. To me, it is heaven sent and I enjoy it. It is just rain, it will never stop me doing anything and you will never hear me complain about it. I cannot bear now to hear people complaining about the rain and calling it filthy weather. In fact, I cannot bear to hear people talking about the weather at all, it is just weather and we have a wonderful variety of it in England! The sun in Spain seemed to be a fascinating pull, but when every day was the same, that unending burning heat with no break could be very exhausting. Trying to sleep at night from May to September, I had a fan running all night right on my face, as it felt like I might have died from the lack of air—the heat was so stifling.

It is, without doubt, infinitely hotter down in the very south. Some friends in the UK rang and asked if they could come and stay one August, and as they had lived near Alicante for a couple of years, I didn't want to insult their intelligence by warning them how hot it was in August, presuming they would know and not mind. I usually recommended that people stayed away in July and August. When they arrived, however, they were staggered by the heat and hardly knew what to do with themselves. My friend had put on about 3 stones in weight since I had seen her last and this didn't help. In addition, we had a house full of people and children as well at the time, which I hadn't known about when they had first rung.

After 3 days, they begged me to try and get them on a flight home, as they couldn't stand the heat or the children. I did try but the only flights available were about £600. They ended up going out every day and finding trees to sit under. They asked me why I hadn't warned them and said that it had not been anywhere near that hot further up country. We were, after all, not far from Morocco.

In fact in the winter months, if it did rain heavily and the rivers filled with water, it was such a rare sight to see a river with any water in it that dozens of the people in the village would pile down to just stand and look at it or congregate at the top of the village looking down. Sometimes it would become a raging torrent, carrying with it all the waste and rubbish that had accumulated along with the dead goats that had died whilst out grazing. It was certainly very cleansing and the air would be so much fresher and cooler. It would also be great fun walking along the river banks and seeing dozens of frogs and toads that appeared, seemingly from nowhere.

Out Riding Our Beautiful Horse

Riding was an amazing experience; there were miles of tracks and dry river beds linking village to village and you could ride for hours without seeing anybody. I remember a German guy from a nearby village telling me some years later that he had been out for a walk in a remote part of the river bed when my daughter came round the bend on our white horse, her blond hair flowing. He thought he was having a vision.

It could be pretty unnerving out in the wilds sometimes. I was riding one day and went round a bend in the river bed. There in front of me was what looked like a group of bandits, about a dozen men with big mops of hair and beards and all with knives in their hands. I took one look at them, turned my horse and rode off as fast as I could. It was a long way before I looked back. They were all staring at me. No doubt they realised I was scared stiff. Later, I learned that they were a group of local men looking for wild asparagus! I was once taken out to find some; it's all a bit of a secret where they are. Rather like mushrooms in England, people are reluctant to tell you where they grow. Why they bother is beyond me, however. I found them stringy and small and a bunch of thick succulent asparagus in the market only cost £1 at the time and tasted much better.

It was nice to visit friends on horseback. Some people pressed me to visit them and it was a pleasure to do so. Everybody was very kind to us and many people invited us into their homes, offering us food and drinks. I tried to give some families as much healing as possible when they needed it as a way of doing my bit for the community.

Visiting Henry

One young man Henry, who was half Spanish and half Indian, had built himself a one room dwelling way outside a nearby village and several miles down a steep dirt track. When you arrived near his dwelling, you had to climb down or slide down a very steep bank, crawl under some trees, over some bushes and there he lived. No water, electricity or mod cons of any description. He had a bed, a couple of chairs and a log stove to cook on. He had had some unhappy personal experiences and had withdrawn from normal life. He seemed to be barely surviving. He had bought the land and had struggled to build the house, as he called it, because of the difficulty in getting materials there. He had no transport. He wasn't working and appeared to be living on thin air. The spot he had built on was paradise, though.

We all visited each other and I was happy to prepare him a meal sometimes. I enjoyed riding over to see him. I let Tammy loose and she loved having a good feed of beautiful succulent grass. He had a lot of grapes growing on the hillside behind his house. The hill was at about 45 degrees angle, really hard to climb up it. He had other fruit and nut trees, but also had quite a lot of scorpions.

One day he called in and excitedly told me he had found water. You would think he had found gold. He wanted me to go and see it straight away, so I rode over. Leaving Tammy to graze, I followed him, scrambling with difficulty down a very steep slope, half on my bottom, until we reached the dry river bed. We pushed through undergrowth, brambles and bushes and came to a rocky area, where he had dug a hole about 2 feet across in the dry river bed and found a drop of water. He had made a tiny pool and it filled up to give him at least half a bucket. I guess if you have no water, even half a bucket of muddy water full of frogs and toads is enough to make you ecstatic. I found it difficult to share his euphoria. He talked enthusiastically about how he would bring this water up to the house. Presently, in order to wash, he had rigged up a shower outside his home using a bucket with holes in the bottom on top of a pole.

My youngest daughter came with me one day to visit Henry, but she was appalled at his lack of conveniences. Her sister and brother had been brought up in Somerset amongst building chaos. We had spent 8 years building our house there. They had climbed ladders for 3 and half years and once when we had finally put in the stairs, they both fell headlong down them within 2 weeks and had to be taken to hospital with concussion.

When Pamela was born, the house was all finished and comfortable so she wasn't used to such primitive conditions. I could tell she was appalled at the dwelling itself, but I became acutely embarrassed when he took us both to show us his grapes and Pamela looked at the 45 degree hill which we had to climb up to get to the grapes. She collapsed on the grass in complete hysterics. I tried to get her to pull herself together but it was hopeless; it was difficult for me not to laugh too. He wanted to know what was wrong with her and I said I had no idea. She just could not believe that anybody could live in such a place. He may not have had any mod cons, but he lived in the most spectacular place with stunning views of hills and mountains all round him. It was utterly peaceful.

To earn some money, he tried his hand at busking in Torremolinos; he took his guitar and sat on some busy steps right in the centre of town but kept getting moved on, he didn't earn a peseta. He was an educated man; he had been working in a bank in London for some years. I understood how he felt; he just didn't want the hassle of the rat race at that time.

A Romeria

One day, Henry and I went to a romeria together. Gypsies arrived from all over the area and camped for several days. There were hundreds of beautiful Andalucían horses, all adorned with flowers and ribbons, oxen covered with flowers, magnificent carts elaborately decorated—it is an amazing sight. Riders were dressed in their finery and elegantly pranced about all day and night on horseback, showing off their dressage skills. Others were singing, dancing and playing guitars. There was hot food available and lots to drink. It was one of the most memorable nights of my life. We stayed until about 4 a.m. and it was truly enchanting.

Trying to Sell His Home

After some years, Henry moved up to the north of Spain near his sister to a small village where he opened an art shop. He started advertising his property for sale and asked me if I could help him sell it. He offered me a commission. I frankly could not imagine anybody buying it; it was so small and remote.

The advertisement read: 'A detached house in the country for sale with so much land, grapes, fruit trees, etc. 1 million pesetas.' This was about £5,000 then. It was a ridiculously cheap price for a detached house in the country with quite a bit of land; he must have had about 3 or 4 acres, but I thought it was an excessive price at that time for the small dwelling that it was. I showed a lot of people over the place and sometimes it was hilarious. I had such a laugh about it. People would arrive at my door and I would offer to drive, knowing that most people were paranoid about their cars. They wouldn't risk driving down such a crazy dirt track full of pot holes with drops over the edge.

Most insisted on driving and then when we arrived where we turned off down the track, they were utterly horrified and refused to go any further. Others eventually arrived at the house after driving like snails, looked down the hill and could not believe their eyes. They would be expecting a detached house and it really was no more than a hut. They then had the job of turning the car round where there was nowhere to turn—it was all such a palaver. I much preferred to drive myself, as I knew the track well.

One Sunday, a Spanish couple arrived from Marbella, dressed in matching Marbella sailing club T-shirts. They were driving a brand new silver Mercedes Benz. I told the couple that the track was bad and it would be better if I drove. They looked at the Seat Panda I was driving then and said no. They told me to get in and that we would be fine. We arrived at the turn-off to the track which went sharp left and down in a curve. They drove about 20 yards and stopped. They said the track was appalling and they couldn't possibly drive their car down it.

"We will walk," they said.

I said, "We cannot walk, it is several miles."

"That's fine," they said, "we can walk several miles."

Never mind about me, I thought. I had at the time been cooking lunch for us; I had left my daughter to keep an eye on it. I could see we wouldn't be eating it for hours.

The lady had on a pair of very elegant high-heeled shoes. It was a baking hot summer's day. We all set off to walk down the stony uneven dirt track. We walked about 30 yards and the woman threw a tantrum and said she couldn't walk another step. She hobbled back to the car. They decided the location was utterly impossible and wanted to go home without even bothering to see the house. They tried to back out the way they had come, but this meant backing on a curve and going back up the steep slope. He tried again and again and couldn't manage it. Time was going on, and I was getting very fed up with the pair. They were arguing like crazy, calling each other all sorts of names and shouting their heads off.

In the end, he had no alternative but to drive straight on, as he couldn't turn around with a sheer drop on one side and a bank on the other. I have never been in a car that was driven so slowly. We crawled along the track in his immaculate silver Mercedes and it took an interminable time to get there. We were sweltering in the heat, and they were ranting and raving about how outrageous it all was.

When we finally got to the spot where you could look down at the 'house', they exploded. I couldn't blame them really, but what could they expect for a million pesetas? It wasn't my fault that the description in the paper was so elaborate, I was only trying to help. I do not know how many turns he did to get that car round; I usually did it in my Panda by half driving up a bank and narrowly missing a big tree. I'd got it down to a fine art.

I had had enough of these two by now and I sat in the back and let them scream and shout and then we crawled back down the track and I was glad to get back to my lunch. The whole saga had lasted 3 hours. I could have done it in 40 minutes. From that moment on, I insisted on driving would-be purchasers or we didn't go. In the end, unfortunately for me, a couple who had looked at it directly without my help bought it so I didn't get any commission.

The Animals

The treatment of animals has to be seen to be believed. The first abandoned kitten we rescued there grew into a beautiful ginger tom called Saffy, perfectly healthy and strong. We came home one day and found him dead under the bed. We were so shocked and upset that we called our English neighbour down the road and he confirmed that he had been poisoned. He said he could tell because of his weight, he had been totally dehydrated by the poison. It had happened to all his cats. He told me that the neighbours poisoned cats. I couldn't believe him, it seemed impossible to understand. We were beside ourselves. We are far too sensitive about animals to live in such a place and I have cried more tears than I could imagine possible over the years at what I have seen and experienced.

He went on to explain that this was a normal occurrence there, the people threw poison down everywhere and killed lots of cats. All the cats he had ever owned there had been poisoned. We were horrified, not having ever heard such a thing before, I found it impossible to believe. He buried him for us in the garden. We rescued 11 cats living there, lots of kittens and loved every one so much. Seven of them were poisoned. It broke my heart and I have cried for years about them, each cat meaning so much to us. I tried to have the practice stopped over the years, I ranted at the neighbours, demanding that they stop putting poison down. I went to the town hall and complained bitterly about it. I even went to the police on the coast and denounced the town hall, as throwing poison around is totally illegal. Poison is thrown everywhere to kill rats, cats and also foxes.

A great number of people also suffered from this poisoning, not just us. Many people's dogs were poisoned. One family in a nearby village had 16 cats all poisoned at the same time. The young children in the family were all hysterical. The heartbreak this causes everyone is horrendous and the suffering to the animals themselves is unbearable, as they die a slow and painful death and nothing can be done, as one of our cats went into a veterinary hospital in Malaga for two days but they couldn't save her.

Instead of having female cats and bitches neutered, which costs money, they simply have litters of kittens and puppies non-stop. Then the kittens and puppies are taken to the rubbish tips or onto the hills and left to die in the hot sun. This happened in every village everywhere. Rat poison was thrown carelessly anywhere, even though it is illegal to do so. Rats and mice die, cats eat the poisoned creatures and die horrible deaths. I should know, of the 7 of my cats that were poisoned, 4 of those cats had been neutered at a cost of £240. We took in endless animals; we ended up with 17 cats and 7 dogs.

The foxes were poisoned so that there would be plenty of rabbits for the men to hunt with their guns on a regular basis. Most of the men in the villages got dressed up in their hunting clothes with huge belts round their middles full of bullets, with hooks to hang their rabbits on. It is a big macho thing. Coming home, everyone knows how fabulous you are depending on how many rabbits you have hanging from your belt. They then had a big party cooking their spoils. On one of these hunting trips, two dogs were deliberately shot and killed because they were owned by a member of the opposition party in the town hall who was complaining about the corruption. I was pleased that a few of the younger men who we were friends with were too sensitive to join in.

One of my beautiful cats, Jasmine, completely white, was shot with an air gun and came home limping in agony; she had a pellet embedded in her foot. It was quicker for me to remove it than taker her to the vet and I held her down firmly with one arm whilst I got the pellet out with some tool. I went on the rampage for the culprit who had done it. Children aren't allowed to run around shooting with air guns. They all denied it, of course. I screamed at those I knew had guns—parents bought them for their sons as presents when they are as young as 11 years old—and threatened to denounce them if I ever saw them using one against animals again. I knew those boys and we normally got on well, and they took my chastisement with downcast faces. Nevertheless, if the pellet had hit her head, she would have died. All of our cats had been taken in, rescued by Pamela from rubbish tips. They had been kittens thrown in cactus bushes or left to die in the river beds. I cannot go further into these cases, as the pain is too terrible and it will make extremely depressing reading.

Albercas and Rubbish Tips

The other nightmare hazard which was everywhere for both children and animals were the albercas. These were straight-sided concrete water containers which were very deep in the ground, used for irrigation. The water levels were often half full so that if something or someone fell in, they could not get out. Two children at least in a nearby village died by falling in and not being able to get out, a young child and an 18-year-old. These albercas were often out in the country, well away from a house and calls for help would never be heard. I lost a dog and a cat in this way. I was once walking in the hills with my boxer dog and he was so hot, he tried to jump in one. I had difficulty in preventing him, as I didn't have a lead with me. If he had jumped in, I would not have been able to fish him out, as the water level was very low. They are an extremely dangerous hazard and should be abolished by the European Parliament, and yet every landowner has one.

Rubbish tips abound, although there are directives that these have to be removed. We had a massive rubbish tip, right in the river bed and right near our water supply to the village. It burned day and night, sending out black smoke and a horrible stench and pollution. It was utterly disgusting and dogs and cats would be trying to survive from it by searching for scraps.

Lucy

One day Pamela came home from school and told me to come to the rubbish tip quickly because there was a dog there in a terrible state. She had passed it on the way home. We walked

68

down there to find one of the most pathetic sights I have ever seen—a big dog with no flesh, just bones, with hundreds of ticks covering every inch of its body. It was so weak it couldn't stand, it was sitting amidst all the rubbish. I told Pamela that if we walked away from the dog, it would be dead the next day. We talked to her and she smiled at us despite her suffering, and I realised she was a very sweet dog. I also realised it was a dog I had seen a week or so earlier being screamed at by my neighbour opposite. She chased it away with a broom and I just saw it running round the corner and I hadn't seen it since.

We hardly knew where to begin. We couldn't get hold of her because there was no part of her not covered in hideous ticks. Her long ears were covered in them also. We went home and got a spray to kill them and a bowl of meat and cereals. I always had huge pans of animal food in the kitchen to feed our own and also all the strays. We returned and fed her first as she was utterly starving and almost too weak to eat. When she had finished, we then sprayed her with this insecticide and the poor dog fainted. The insecticide must have caused the ticks to dig into her flesh and caused her excruciating pain. She came around and we carefully tied some rope round her neck and got her to her feet and walked her back to our garden very slowly. We had a huge oil drum which was clean and we put it on its side, got some blankets and put her inside. We tied her on a long rope to our horse box, so that she could move about but we could not have her near the house until we had cleaned her up.

We then bathed her very gently with a sponge in an antiseptic solution to start the process of killing the ticks. The only place we could stroke her was the end of her nose. Despite her intense suffering, she was delighted to have been rescued and looked so grateful. We had to feed her small meals often to build her up slowly. It took weeks for all the ticks to fall off and it took 6 months to get her back to a good weight. It was also the talk of the town. I heard my neighbour who had screamed at her and chased her away telling another neighbour what we had done. They seemed amazed. We saved her in the nick of time because the town hall had decided to shoot her the next day to put her out of her misery. She was a hunting dog. She obviously hadn't hunted well and when they don't work properly, they get thrown out and left to starve.

We called her Lucy and I promised her that first day that I would take her to the beach as soon as she was well enough. My boxer just loved the beach, and I kept my word and would take both dogs often for a fabulous run both on the beach and down to open spaces near a golf course. As soon as she was well enough, she came into the house.

We had had her a year, she looked magnificent, a big cream lolloping animal, loving, sweet and affectionate. She got on well with Saul and the cats and was a happy, strong and healthy dog. Then, one day Pamela went off with the two dogs to collect our horse Tammy who had been in a friend's land for the day. On the way home, Lucy ran off. She had a tendency to do that, so Pamela arrived back with Tammy and Saul and then set off out again to look for Lucy. We spent the next 10 days looking for her, we walked for miles and miles over the hills, calling and asking everybody if they had seen her. We suspected somebody may have stolen her as she looked so good.

Then a child came up to me one day and looked at me very sadly. I asked him what was wrong and he looked at me with big eyes and said Lucy had been found at the bottom of an alberca, where she had drowned. She had obviously jumped in to have a drink and couldn't get out. He said nobody had wanted to tell us because they knew we would be upset. What a terrible end after all the hard work. We were devastated and could only console ourselves with the thought that we had given her a year of happiness and love.

Animals have to work or they are useless. The cruelty to animals is shameful. Even when they have a home, they are fed on stale white bread and not much else and are always thin and hungry.

Basically, it may stem back to the time when frankly the people themselves were so poor they barely had food for themselves. Those times are over now and there is sufficient social security for everyone to eat properly. The majority of the women are extremely overweight, so there is no need for animals to be kept so very hungry and badly treated.

There were one or two people who genuinely did care about their animals. One wonderful lady in the village found her precious Siamese cat dead one day and went quite berserk. She rampaged round the village like a mad thing, wanting to know who had thrown down poison and she kept on until she found the culprit. She was devastated and poured her heart out to me, saying she could never go through such pain again. She never wanted another cat. I was pleased that at least somebody else cared apart from us.

Some Are More Caring

I was heartened by what appeared to be much more sensitivity in the children. Various children arrived at our house with animals and birds in poor states of health for me to either treat with healing or take in and look after. The mayor's wife and daughter arrived one day with a tiny chick that had fallen down a flight of stairs and it died as they handed it to me. The child was sobbing and I was pleased that she cared. We took it into my garden and buried it properly. I took all opportunities when I could to try and teach the children to love and respect animals and birds.

One day, a group of children came running to my door and told me to hurry to the church. A baby peregrine falcon had fallen from its nest from the top of the church. When I got there, it looked dead, flattened on the ground. I must say the healing that bird received was the most instant and spectacular I have ever seen. It simply revived instantly and got up, pulled itself up to its full height. It was huge even though it was a baby. I hardly knew what to do with it. We took it indoors and started to feed it on pieces of chicken on the end of a fork, which he took happily. He lived in the kitchen, hopping about from place to place.

After a week of eating very well and thriving, I decided I had to sort something else out. I got in touch with the local government office for the environment and was pleased to be told that they could help me. They despatched a gentleman with a van and he explained in great detail how they would rear it and teach it to fend for itself. He was most anxious to reassure me that it would be very carefully looked after. He invited me to go anytime I wanted to visit and he also wrote me a letter afterwards thanking me for rescuing the bird and taking care of it. I was very impressed and greatly relieved that this kind of help was available.

In fact, there is a strong movement growing in Spain regarding conservation and bird and animal protection. There were new laws put in place while I was there to prevent the shooting of birds, and only the fines of £500 seemed to deter people. Even so, young children are taught from an early age to shoot anything that moves and they seemed reluctant to stop. I threatened some young boys that I would report them for shooting swallows and swifts and whilst I was around, they were scared to do so but I am sure as soon as I left the village to go out, the guns would come out and they would carry on. There are plenty of laws in Spain, but nobody takes any notice of them.

I was disgusted and outraged when I first arrived to live there that Greenpeace were not allowed to dock in Malaga. They were turned away. Some while later, they were given permission to dock.

Some years later when I was teaching English to some lovely families on the coast, I would tell them some of the stories about the treatment of the animals in the villages and they were genuinely horrified and embarrassed. Almost every family I taught had a dog, there were quite a few poodles, one had a boxer, another had an Alsatian with his own trailer his owner had built especially for him, to be towed behind the car, as the car was full up with children. All the dogs were utterly loved, pampered and cared for, although nobody had a cat. I taught in a lot of homes, and none of the families I knew had even been into the interior and seemed to think that anyone who lived more than a mile inland was a savage. It was like two different and separate worlds.

Going Berserk

I don't lose my temper very often, I used to before I started to meditate and this calmed me down dramatically. I did lose it, however, with the mayor and over the animals.

In a nearby village, I had to wait every day for the college bus to arrive in order to pick up Pamela. On the days I was working the whole day through, she had to walk home. The bus would pull up alongside the rubbish bins, which were all open and overflowing, stinking and disgusting. A couple of dozen cats and kittens were always rummaging for scraps through the sacks, poor little scraps of skin and bone. I started taking bowls of meat and rice and found the cleanest spot on the ground and laid it down on paper for them.

One day, as I was waiting for the bus to arrive, a huge lady waddled out of her front gate about 20 yards away. I suddenly lost my cool; there she was with her neat little house and garden, a big, swollen, fat, overstuffed woman, ignoring all these starving creatures on her doorstep. I screamed my head off at her and asked her what the hell the matter was with her and everybody else in the godforsaken village. How could she live here and just ignore all these starving animals right outside her door, how could she stuff her face and leave them to die, and didn't anybody in this place have a heart or any feelings? She was obviously quite shocked by this outburst and her father, who I was quite friendly with, never spoke to me again.

A Severely Neglected Horse

On another occasion, Sandra and I had been to the feed mill to buy Tammy several sacks of feed. On our way home, we were driving through some back streets which were a short cut and we came across a piece of waste land. There, tethered on a short piece of rope, was the most pitiful sight—a horse so thin, it was a mass of bones, the flesh between its ribs had sunk in, bones stuck out and it was crippled. It looked as though it had a broken leg and back. I felt an immense rage welling up inside me. As we were looking at it in horror, a man on horseback was riding towards us and passed us just 2 metres away. He was a magnificent sight, dressed in beautiful clothes and was seated on a huge fat black stallion glistening with health. I went up to him and asked him to stop and talk to me about this horse and asked him if he knew who it belonged to. He said he didn't know, didn't slow down and then simply ignored us and the horse we were stood by and rode on by.

I went completely nuts, I started screaming my head off at this man, asking him how on earth he could ride past the animal dying on its feet, while he was sat on such a beautiful horse? How could he? And why on earth was he not doing something about this, he obviously lived nearby! He continued to ignore me with a pained expression on his face, but I was walking alongside him. I shouted at him and asked him why nobody cared and why wasn't he sorting it out and what the hell was the matter with the people of this country, how could they just stand by and do nothing to relieve the suffering of animals? As he continued to ignore me, I swore at him profusely, having learned how to very well.

We went over to the car and found some plastic bags and filled them with some suitable feed. A lot of the feed we had on board had to be soaked for 24 hours before it could be eaten, such as the whole oats, barley and sugar beet. We placed it on the ground in front of her, but she was so weak and lifeless that she didn't seem that interested. She did slowly start to eat and we went back and found some water and a container.

We then went off into town and made some enquiries. We found the nearest vet and went in and spoke to him. We told him all about it and begged him to do something, get in touch with the appropriate authorities, anything. He waffled on about this and that and basically wouldn't do anything. We then went to the local Ministry of Health and I ranted on at them insisting that they did something to help. They gave me a dozen reasons why they couldn't do anything.

Finally, we went to the police, I was still in a rage and I asked them what they were going to do about it and or what I could do about it. The guy on the desk was a huge laid back bloke and smiled faintly. I could see he didn't give a damn. I got very heated and asked for some paper work and said I wanted to denounce the owner of the horse and take him to court. He then looked at me with some sympathy and told me that the owner was a gypsy and he was in jail and that I would be well advised not to take that course of action. It would be very unwise.

"What then are you going to do about it?" I insisted, but it soon became apparent that he would do nothing.

We decided the only option was to simply steal the horse and take it back home. We checked back on the animal and were pleased to see it was at least eating and then made our way home. When we got back, a couple of neighbours were in the street and we related the sorry tale. I was still seething. I told them we needed some help and were going down that night to pick it up with our horse box and bring it back. They got very cross with me and said I had to stop running round the place, interfering in other peoples' business and under no circumstances would they allow me to bring back some sick horse to the village where their children could be in danger of contracting a disease. We all argued the toss, but they told me straight that if we stole the horse, they would report us to the police.

The next day, we went back to see the animal and it had gone. We looked for her on foot and in the car and couldn't find her. We asked a few people and they said they knew nothing about it. We looked for her over a few days and decided that perhaps the vet, the Ministry of Health or the police had in fact done something after all, even had her put down. We thought maybe she had died and been removed. We had to get over it. All I could do was pray that if she was still alive, she would be helped.

It was probably 2 years later when an English couple knocked on my door. They had arrived in the village hoping to buy a house there and the town hall had sent them down to me. They were living in an even more remote village much higher up in the mountains, which could be seen in the far distance, especially at night when all the lights were shimmering. I invited them in and made them tea and we all sat chatting.

Somehow the subject came round to the horse and I told them a bit about it.

"Strange," they said, "we had a similar experience," and told me a bit about it. We compared notes and it turned out we were talking about the same horse and it was them who had removed her. They had been several steps ahead of us and had already tracked down the gypsy's family. They took bales of hay to feed her but the gypsies took the hay away from her and gave it to their other animals and wouldn't feed her, saying she was too crippled to bother with. After several visits, they struck a deal. They flatly refused to give the gypsies money but ended up swapping her for a saddle.

They then went off and found a stable to rent in the town, hired a truck and took her away—that would have been the evening after we had come across her. They gave her a thick bed of straw, got the vet out who confirmed that she had a broken leg and back, wormed her, fed her, loved her and nursed her back to health. It was utterly extraordinary that these people should have come to our house and we heard all this for we had wondered ever since what had happened to her. That visit was surely arranged from above.

Stories like that abounded everywhere. I met people of various nationalities who were involved in helping animals, French, German, Dutch, Danish and of course English. It was often overwhelming. I knew of a lady of 75 who ended up with about 35 dogs and cats and could barely cope. Another German lady living out in the wilds somewhere had collected about 30 dogs. The poor lady died and nobody found her for weeks, by which time the dogs had half eaten her and each other.

In the end, trying to live there and cope with it all on a daily basis was very exhausting and foreigners found it difficult and depressing, many giving up in the end and returning home as they got worn down by it.

The Power of the Mayor

After the unpleasant incident with the town hall and the mayor over my land, I got in touch with my lawyer. He came to the village several times to have discussions with the mayor and I also went a few times and tried to discuss the matter with him. He wasn't having any of it. Without doubt, he would have deeply regretted ever trying to mess with me, because I wasn't scared of him and I certainly wasn't about to give in and have a house built in my garden. My documents were totally legal. When a new Escritura is made, it had by law then to hang in the town hall for a period of one month and if there were any discrepancies in the details, then that was the time to sort them out. If no complaint was made during that time, then the registration of the Escritura went ahead in the Land Registry office. All this had been done, but the mayor insisted he hadn't read the details of my Escritura, the simple reason being that he couldn't read or write. He had a secretary who came on a regular basis who could, but in any event, my papers stood, totally legal.

One family had owned our house for 40 years and the land in question had been bought by them from the mayor's father-in-law. Everybody knew the truth of this but truth didn't count for much in this village, the mayor had a stranglehold on the place. Mayors have a great deal of power in Spain and fortunately, there are many who are perfectly honest. Pamela was friends with a girl whose father was a mayor in a nearby village. They were a very nice family, had a modest home and her father, as well as being the mayor, worked driving a bus. He was very sweet to me at a much later date when I was flying round a bend on one of the dirt track roads in a rush to get to the hospital to see my daughter and smashed right into his bus. There wasn't much damage, just a couple of dents. He knew me and knew where I was going and just let the matter drop, which was a great relief.

My lawyer even suggested buying my land from the mayor, which I was not at all pleased about when he told me afterwards. I would not have agreed to it anyway, but he was trying to resolve the dispute in any way he could. The mayor insisted that at any moment he was going to reclaim the land and build a house on it. It was a nightmare hanging over my head and it was spoiling my life; I didn't need all the hassle. My lawyer was doing his best to prevent this happening and frankly, I was a nervous wreck about it all.

I thought of my Spanish friend in Taunton, who had been teaching me Spanish. She was one of 13 children and came from Leon in the north of Spain. One of her brothers bought a house in that area, paid £45,000 for it, and after all the paperwork was completed, the local mayor announced that the land was his and grabbed the house and land and despite trying to fight him with lawyers, they lost it all. The way people, me included, go over to Spain and just buy property without knowing what they are doing is so crazy, there is a great deal of corruption and also anyone who cannot speak the language is at a great disadvantage.

I recently met a woman living in a Devon village who had been left a flat on the Spanish coast by her aunt. This woman had no idea what to do with it, did nothing, didn't even go there to see it because she couldn't cope with it and then found out that the warden of the flats had broken into her flat, changed the lock and was renting it out and taking the profit. Still, she didn't go, had no lawyer and had no idea what to do about it. I urged her to get an English-speaking lawyer and have it sorted out, but she didn't want to. I offered to put her in touch with my own lawyer but she refused.

I Join a Club

When I initially found myself alone in the early days, my English neighbour took me along to an English-speaking club in Malaga, where an interesting mixture of people of all different nationalities met and conversed. The club usually met in a

Chinese restaurant next to the beach, and it made a pleasant evening. Outings were arranged to various places of interest and buses to Gibraltar were regularly organised. Several Spanish people joined the club in order to practise speaking English. What I did find amazing, however, was meeting English people, Germans, French and other Europeans who had lived in Spain for many years—some as many as 20 years and who could not speak Spanish. How on earth could they manage to cope with everything? They often ended up paying a lot of money to their lawyer or a gestor, who is like an accountant who deals with paperwork. Thousands upon thousands of pounds were given to these people when it was totally unnecessary.

Take for instance the residence permit. You could pay a gestor to do the paperwork for you or you could simply walk into the police station and start the process there. The cost was minimal. A friend of mine ended up paying about £7,500 to a lawyer for getting two residence permits for her and her husband because they didn't speak Spanish. It also took forever to get it all done. It cost us about £20. We went to our local police station, made enquiries, filled in some forms, did what we were told regarding a few bits of paper and then went back and collected our residence permits. However, that had to be done in Spanish. This is why it is so important to speak the language; it saves you a lot of money. Of course the laws are changing all the time so these need to be checked. Taxes do have to be organised by the gestor.

Cringing at Tourists

We witnessed some cringing displays by foreigners arrogantly speaking their own language and expecting everyone to understand them. I was in a gift shop in Benalmadena when in walked an American woman, and in a very loud voice she said, "Does anybody in this joint speak English?"

As nobody answered, she said, "Oh my God, what kind of a dump is this?" I might have offered to help her if she hadn't been so rude.

Sandra was getting on a bus one day in Malaga and an English woman in front of her was giving the bus driver a hard time. "Now look here," she said, "I bought this ticket to go Marbella but I made a mistake and now I don't want to go there,

I want to go to Torremolinos instead. Now I don't know how to change the ticket or how to get my money back and it's just not good enough. What are you going to do about it? What I need now is a return ticket to Torremolinos."

"Que?" was his answer.

Whilst shopping one day in a supermarket in Fuengirola, a group of people were giving the till girl a hard time. They wanted salt and pepper and couldn't find them. What did they do? Shouted and then shouted louder, "SALT, PEPPER!" Over and over, they shouted, "SALT, PEPPER!" I was appalled and embarrassed and felt so sorry for the girl trying to serve them. Some people don't seem to have heard of dictionaries.

I was fortunate to have 2 excellent teachers in Somerset and chose to have a one to one private class with both of them. I asked the English lady to push me hard and she certainly did that. I had homework and I made myself study. I studied for hours. She also started me on Don Quijote, a Spanish classic written in 1537 by Cervantes whilst he was in jail. There were a lot of ancient words but what was fascinating was the insight into life at that time. It was about a crazy man who was obsessed by wars and fighting and he took himself off on his old horse to start battle himself with whoever got in his way, including some windmills.

It is a very amusing and interesting book and is well worth reading, copies are available also in English. I seem to have been reading it for years and still haven't actually finished it.

Some people can find themselves in terrible difficulties. I know a lady now of 83 whose husband has just died; she is halfway up a mountain, cannot drive, cannot speak Spanish and has no idea how to pay any bill whatsoever. She has been there for 25 years. She is having to rely on neighbours to help her out.

It seems to happen that people congregate with their own nationalities in areas. There are whole regions that are predominantly English and others that are predominantly German and so on. These people then just mainly mix with each other and hardly have anything to do with anyone else.

Sandra Leaves Us

Two years after we arrived, a girlfriend of Sandra's came for a holiday. A few days before this girl was due to return home, Sandra suddenly announced that she was going to return to

England to live and she asked me to get her a flight on the same plane going back with her friend. She said she missed all her friends. I was devastated. The family had fallen apart and I had lost 3 people from my family within 2 years. The shock of her unexpected departure affected me very badly. Two days later, I had my first very bad asthma attack and had to go to hospital.

Javier

Probably because I was alone with only Pamela for company, and feeling very sorry for myself, I became attracted to a young man called Javier in the village. Then one summer, we had a close friend, her partner and his 3 children staying with us for a couple of weeks. This particular night, we were enjoying the feria. Everybody was dancing in the square, and a dear friend of mine from another village came up to me and pointing to Javier said, "Do you realise that that guy over there is in love with you? He has not taken his eyes off you all night."

I hadn't realised and was surprised but pleased and hoped that some relationship could develop between us, even though he was much younger than me. In the early hours of the morning, we all went home. My friends all went to bed and before I turned in, there was a knock at the front door. I opened the door and in came Javier with two of his friends from the village, who I knew very well.

We also had a house full of German students staying at that time as well as our friends and every bedroom was full. I made them all some refreshments. Somehow, Javier and I ended up disappearing together leaving his two friends downstairs, and after a short time, they decided to go round the house and search for us. They entered 5 bedrooms, putting the lights on and waking everybody up, shocking them all in the process.

Then outside, Javier's brother and some friends were hammering on the front door looking for him and shouting their heads off, calling his name over and over. It was about 4 a.m. My daughter had got up and told them to go away so they then found a huge pole and were trying to batter the door down. The mayhem, to which I confess I was oblivious, woke the whole house up and we eventually went downstairs to find a lot of irate people in the sitting room, especially my daughter. Javier let himself out and went off with the men waiting for him.

I then received a thorough dressing down from everyone. My daughter said my behaviour was deplorable and I should be thoroughly ashamed of myself. She was about 13 at the time, and she stalked off to bed in a huff. Then my friends said they were afraid that the boys who had burst in their rooms had taken flash photographs of them all in the nude with no sheets over them and would later supply the local football team with copies. The German students said the noise and scandal was an outrage and it would all be very bad for my reputation as a host for the academy students. They stiffly informed me that when the owner heard about this, he would no doubt never let me have students again.

Frankly, I was feeling pretty happy and thought everybody lacked a sense of humour. However, I apologised to all and sundry, tried to calm my daughter down and we all went back to bed. I was more concerned about the battering my front door had received than anything else, but it still seemed to be on its hinges. It was all a bit embarrassing, and I hoped the incident would blend into the general frivolity of the annual feria and that would be the end of it. I wasn't very pleased to find some of my geraniums outside all broken in pieces.

There was much worse to come, unfortunately. From the very beginning when we first bought the house, one lady in particular had seemed to take a shine to me and we had become good friends. Frani had always been pleased to see me when I arrived in the village to stay over the years. Once I lived there, we continued to be friends, visited each other and occasionally went out together. Regretfully, she was Javier's mother.

A couple of days later, I sauntered into the village. There were a lot of people about, the feria was still going on, and I sat on a wall to take in the scene and along came Frani. I smiled and said hello and she didn't answer. I spoke again thinking she hadn't heard me, she ignored me again, so I said, "Is something wrong?" completely forgetting about the fiasco at my house a couple of nights earlier, in which both her sons had been involved. It had been too much to expect that she hadn't been told, news travelled like lightening in those villages.

She then went nuts, screaming abuse at me, calling me all the names under the sun, using foul language, shouting that I had tricked her son and taken advantage of him because he was drunk. I would have been amused by that last comment if I hadn't been so shocked. I was stunned by her venom and before I realised what was happening, she started beating me about the head with her mop handle, smacking me very hard round the head and body. She had landed quite a few blows before I sprung to my defence. I then grabbed the mop handle and we were both grappling with it. She let go and picked up a bucket of water to throw over me. I ran after her, and she scurried away and locked herself inside her gate, still screaming abuse at me the whole time. I turned away, realising that at least a dozen women had been watching the scene.

I was utterly shocked and humiliated and feeling very sore. I went round the corner and sat down on a step and cried my eyes out. The only person who came to comfort me was a young German student. He was very kind and sat with me for half an hour until I felt recovered enough to walk home. The next day I was black and blue, covered in bruises around my eyes, face, ribs, hips and legs. I hadn't been up long when Javier was knocking at my door. He came in and said that we could not see each other again and was about to leave immediately. I asked him if he knew what his mother had done the previous day. I told him about it and showed him my bruises. He was absolutely stunned as though he couldn't believe it. No doubt there were some tense moments in his house around that time. It was some months later that I heard from a friend that his mother had threatened to commit suicide if he saw me again.

He was about 30 at the time but these mothers have their offspring in a stranglehold.

An Astonishing Turn of Events

I was totally unprepared for what happened soon after. A large hole in the cement floor of Tammy's stable was gradually getting worse and I didn't want her to hurt herself, so I got a couple of guys to mix some cement and get some rubble and redo it. I was helping them when suddenly down the hill ran about a dozen children, all calling my name at the tops of their voices. They all excitedly poured into the house and told me that a television crew was in the village making a film and they wanted to interview me. They would be at my door in 10 minutes.

I was wearing jeans spattered in cement, a raggy old T-shirt and dirty trainers. I had cement on my face and hands. There was pandemonium. I had to fly round getting washed, changed and trying to clear up the house. I presumed that they were coming to look at my pottery so I hastily got out some of my best teapots and sculptures and arranged them on a table. I put on clean jeans and T-shirt and ran downstairs. Pamela was screaming at me to get changed again, saying that I could not possibly go on television wearing jeans and that I had to put on a suit. I was shrieking that there was no time and we were both running round in a panic.

Then they arrived. Twelve people poured into my front room, people with lights and cameras. Several neighbours arrived and walked in to watch. I had had no time to get anxious about the actual interview, which was just as well. They told me that they were doing a film about various interesting people in the village and I had been recommended. I showed them my pots and said well this is what I do, here is a nice selection. "No," they said, "we aren't interested in your pottery." They had already interviewed another potter; there were about 5 of us making pots in the village. "It is your work as a healer and therapist that we want you to talk about."

Whilst flying about changing my clothes, I had been mentally thinking of a few things to say in Spanish about my pottery. Now, it was a different subject. I had no time whatever to collect my thoughts. The cameras started and I had a microphone in my face. I asked her not to talk too quickly.

The young lady presenter began asking me questions about my work. My neighbour had told her about it; I had been helping both her and her husband and lots more people besides. I was pretty nervous and praying that I would be able to understand and answer easily. She asked lots of questions and I seemed to manage OK. There was just one comment at the end I had to ask her to repeat, which was rather embarrassing. She was very sweet. It may have lasted 10 minutes or so. They then all left and with great relief, I went back to the cementing.

I Am Inundated

I thought no more about it. I presumed we would all be told when it was due to go out. They had come on a Tuesday. The following Sunday, at 9 a.m., there was a knock at my front door. Pamela and I were still in bed. I put on a wrap and popped down to see who it was. I opened the door and there standing outside were 9 people. "Yes," I enquired, "can I help you?"

"We have come for appointments with you," they said. "We have hired a minibus." It seemed the film had been made and gone out on local television the previous night. I was aghast. How was I supposed to deal with 9 people all arriving at once? I normally booked people in, each consultation lasting about an hour.

I was half asleep and to stall them for a few moments, I asked them if they had made prior appointments, knowing perfectly well they didn't. They just smiled and said no. I had to leave them in the street whilst I got dressed, warned Pamela that there would be a crowd of people downstairs when she got up, and let them in. I had first used a bedroom to give treatments in, but after a young man tried to kiss me and some other man gave me a too-close hug, I had since been using the sitting room. Also, after these occasions, I asked my neighbour to come in when I had a male client if I was alone in the house.

A consultation needed to be private; I wondered what on earth I was going to do with so many people. I had to get extra chairs from the kitchen, gave them all magazines to look at, offered them all glasses of water and then took one at a time into a study off the sitting room. With so many of them, it took most of the day. Some of them went up to the bar to get some food, others sat in the street on a wall. As most of the village knew everything that went on as it went on, minute by minute, everybody knew by this time that they had arrived and the streets were full of curious people taking an interest and talking to the visitors. Details of these and other healings and consultations are described in my books Divine Communication and Spiritual Appreciation.

This was the beginning of the most extraordinary period of my working life. It lasted intensely for 6 months before it eased off. I have done all kinds of work in my life, changing direction several times. I went to grammar school and studied French and German at A level and later took a secretarial course. In London, I worked in the Swiss Bank, using French shorthand, and then worked for Mitsubishi where I did French translations and learned Japanese. I was also studying Spanish there, as they employed somebody from the Spanish Embassy to come and teach us. After that, I ran my brother's travel business in the Strand. A year in the Bahamas followed, working as an Executive Secretary for a top luxury hotel.

Back in Somerset, I helped my husband with his garage whilst building a house in our spare time. I was the general dogsbody, running customers around, picking up vehicles, collecting parts and paint, doing the books and answering the telephone. At the same time, I also began training as a potter, did my O and A levels in ceramics at Taunton College of Art and set myself up with my own pottery equipment. I later trained to be a yoga teacher with the British Wheel of Yoga, then qualified as a healer with the National Federation of Spiritual Healers. I had been working as a healer and yoga teacher for many years before we bought the house in Spain.

Interesting Characters

Through a friend in the village, I was introduced to the husband of a very well-known and wealthy heiress. He was an interesting and handsome man, an artist of mixed Vietnamese and Oriental background. He had met his wife in Morocco where she had visited an art exhibition he had on display. He had the prefix 'Prince' and although titles did not impress me, I was curious to know where he was the prince of. Our mutual friend told me that his wife had bought him the title from some obscure part of Cambodia. .

I found the stories he regaled me with about his life simply mind-boggling. They lived a life of such excesses that after she died, he went into the desert in Morocco and lived amongst tribes for some years. According to him, she once bought him a Ferrari for his birthday, when he already had one, plus several other expensive cars and he took it back. She always carried with her an enormous trunk full of lavish and expensive jewellery and would often just give an astonished maid a beautiful diamond ring. They would travel constantly and on arrival, would have the entire place they were renting completely redecorated and refurbished at huge expense.

I just remember that when I was 15, I thought of getting a little Saturday morning job whilst still at school. This heiress and her family owned the worst paying shops anywhere around and my mother forbade me from working there. I recall staff rioting because of the appalling wages.

Paul

Around this time, we decided to have a beautiful patio built in the garden of large terracotta tiles. There was a large mound of solid rock to one side that I hadn't been able to do anything with and I had this dug up and made into a raised paved area. I employed Paul, a young English guy who owned what was basically a goat shed, which he had bought from his parents—they had inherited it from an eccentric aunt. It had a bit of land and he was trying to make the place into a dwelling. This was where we had first kept our horse when we arrived. He mainly lived in England but came over to Spain for several months at a time.

We made friends with him, and we all went out socially on a number of occasions with him, including one wonderful night when we all swam in the sea at midnight. We then went on to a night-club where somebody pushed me into the swimming pool with all my clothes on. As it was winter, I was wearing jeans and a jumper and I was astonished how difficult it was to swim back to the edge of the pool, I was so weighed down with heavy wet clothes. People were getting excited and Paul and Sandra all ended up in the pool and we had a lot of fun. It wasn't so comfortable though, driving home with sopping wet cold clothes.

Another memorable evening we spent with him was great fun. He had employed a couple of Hungarian guys to help him with his cottage and they had invited us to a meal at their place halfway down the mountain. It was basically a building site at the time, a very brave planned project of trying to build a large house on the side of very steep hill. They had a lot of problems with walls falling down and endless failed attempts to dig for water. That particular night, they had made a fire outdoors and cooked us some wonderful goulash, which we ate perched on stones, with glasses of wine, under the stars. They had rigged up some Rolling Stones music and some lights in the trees and it was all quite magical. Some incredibly strong Turkish coffee finished off the evening.

Paul didn't have much work at that time and giving him my patio job seemed like a good idea. However, he charged me more than a Spanish wage and started much later and finished much earlier than the locals. It took him several days and it was at a time when I was extremely busy with treatments. One day, in between clients, I went outside to see how he was getting on, and he was doubled up with back pain, hands pressed on the wall, unable to move. He asked me for a treatment but I wasn't able to help him immediately, as I had someone waiting to see me. When I had finished, I went outside to find him in the same position. I gave him some treatment and his back eased up, and after a while he was able to continue working.

At the end of the job, he handed me the bill and as I was giving him the money, I suggested we could deduct the cost of the treatment which I had given him. I had just made him a mug of tea and he got very angry, flung the tea across the kitchen, took the money and left. I hadn't thought it unreasonable to suggest charging him for my work. After all, I had been paying him for his work and that particular day, I still paid him the same, even though I was working for him some of the time! The thought crossed my mind that I should have left him glued to the wall! We didn't see him again for a few months.

The garden was looking beautiful. I planted an apricot tree and had made flower beds which were full of geraniums of all kinds. Everybody offered me cuttings and they were like bushes, large and pretty. Jack had made a beautiful stone patio at one side of the garden in front of the kiln room, which was next to the stable. There had been a barbecue of sorts when we bought the house. I painted it and we enjoyed many meals outside and invited lots of friends.

Taking Care of Tammy

I used the upper garden which was at the side and back of the house for Tammy. We had our horsebox parked there and I was able to tether her to that and feed her there with hay. Feeding Tammy was an interesting challenge. I had found two feed mills which pretty much sold everything I could want. I was able to buy oats, barley, bran, beans, maize and sugar beet. There wasn't much hay as we know it, the bales available were different kinds of straw, grown in the north, where rain was more plentiful. I bought them anyhow and she enjoyed eating them.

One day, I was following a small truck on the narrow dirt track between two villages and I noticed it was laden with bales of some rich-looking leafy grass. I managed to overtake it at some point and pulled in front, flagging him down. He was carrying bales of alfalfa. He told me where his store was, and I was able to order hay and alfalfa in bulk and have it delivered. Alfalfa was extremely nourishing and I was very pleased to get hold of it. It was baled up just the same as hay. In England, alfalfa was sold chopped up and packed in plastic sacks.

She ate all kinds of new foods she had not had before. Her favourite was carob beans. I had actually paid 35 pence for one carob bean in my health food shop in Taunton. Here in the village, there were several carob trees about and they were laden. The beans fell to the ground and covered the earth. They weren't always collected or sold. I used to ride past one particular tree and I simply could not get her to go past, she insisted on stopping for a snack, she loved them. I enquired about them and was able to collect several sacks of them for her, they made a good addition to her diet. The beans were dark brown and about 3 or 4 inches long, crisp and sweet. I used to eat them too. They were used in the U.K. in confectionery as a substitute for chocolate.

I also used to go to the local market as it was closing and was able to collect sacks of vegetables that they didn't want. I would back the car up and they would very kindly load the car up with piles of carrots, cabbage, leeks, tomatoes and anything they couldn't sell. It all helped to supplement her diet. Another food she had were the cane leaves from the river beds. I noticed she loved them, but I was warned not to give her too many of these, especially the new growth, because they might have damaged her eyes. Our American friend also allowed her to go into his finca, where the grass was thick and lush, so she was doing alright.

One day when I picked her up, I noticed she had about 40 enormous black ticks in her mane—they were disgusting. I pulled them out with tweezers, as they were so large, and then bathed her with disinfectant. She had been in a particularly lush area of undergrowth, where there were lots of succulent weeds and obviously lots of horrible ticks. She was tethered all over the place on a 30 metre rope, which gave her plenty of room. She went in various parts of the river, I would find a clearing with lots of grass and she stayed there happily eating until we collected her. There were areas of the river beds which were sheltered and an abundance of grass and plants she liked grew in profusion. I found an area near another village in the river bed where there were masses of good foodstuffs, and I used to drive there in the 4 wheel drive I had and load it up. She particularly loved the wild sticky sweet pea plants which grew everywhere. I gathered piles of it in my arms and took it home.

Sometimes, I would let the children in the village ride her whilst I supervised. I was very careful that they took care of her and also careful that the children weren't hurt. We would go down to the river bed. Sometimes about 12 children came and each child would take it in turns to get on her and have a short ride up and down. They loved it and she seemed to enjoy it, too.

We Need an Enclosed Garden

What I needed, however, was for my land to be enclosed with fencing so that I could let her free, and this was a bone of contention with the mayor. He continued to insist that the land was his so he would not give me permission to fence it. I applied on several occasions and it was constantly rejected. My gardens were open, therefore, for anybody to just walk in.

People did. I caught one guy walking off with a pile of my stuff, I screamed at him but he didn't stop. Other people would walk their goats right through my land, they ate everything in sight. One or two of the mules would escape and walk down into the bottom garden and come and visit Tammy. A horse from the next village escaped constantly and ended up in our garden to visit, stamping on all my plants. I let her stay because I knew she was badly treated where she lived. She would sometimes be around for 2 days before the owner came for her. He then stuck his fingers up her nose to hurt her, then on a short rope hauled her home behind his car. Back at home, the poor creature was then tied outside a building by a rope about a metre long with no food or water.

A lot of different people wanted to buy Tammy. I made it perfectly clear that she was not for sale at any price. One man persisted, however. Every time he saw me, he asked again. I didn't even want him near my horse, as I saw the way he treated his goats, beating them for nothing if they took the wrong path. That man also beat his wife and sons. He wouldn't let his wife out of the house unless he accompanied her. She was not allowed to go into the street to buy bread or food from the vans. He was obviously scared she would run off with one of those people. One day, he had to go to Malaga and the poor woman came into the street to talk to everybody. She was constantly looking over her shoulder in case he should appear. She was so frightened. She eventually became very ill with cancer. One of her sons finally beat their father up in the street one night, and he had to be taken to hospital.

He has since passed into the next world and his wife seems to be well, so perhaps they are all having a bit of peace at last.

The local people could not understand why we had a horse that didn't work. Animals either had to work or they were brutally neglected. It was suggested that we hired her out to be used for work, hauling sacks of produce or whatever. It seemed beyond anybody's comprehension that we could have a horse because we loved her and she was part of our family. We had had her already for about 10 years; we bought her in Somerset when Sandra was 10 years old. Sandra did show jumping, dressage and cross country with her and she had won 59 rosettes. We all rode her and she belonged to us.

We don't agree with selling animals when they are no longer 'of any use'. Some people use horses as though they were bicycles and have no feelings. As I write, we still have her and she is now 33 years old, still strong and healthy.

Trying to Help

Out riding one day, I met an English woman who lived in quite an isolated house outside a village. She had a horse of her own and there was a family crisis back in England, and she had to return to sort it out and stay for a few months. She was trying to sell her horse and asked me if I could help. I went to see my friends at the stables. Miguel then took me to Velez Malaga to meet a friend of his, who he said owned a few horses. We arrived and parked the car and were then walking down a very narrow street of what appeared to be small terraced houses in a very built up area. Miguel knocked at a door and to my amazement, the door opened into quite a large yard, with about 10 stables. There were some very beautiful Andalucían horses, manes about 2 feet long. The two guys started talking their heads off about this horse and that horse, whilst I enjoyed looking at them all.

Miguel's friend Pepe was a gypsy, a big guy with a mop of black hair and extremely good looking. His wife had seen me coming and rushed to his side, ever protective. I was not into trying to steal other peoples' husbands, though the thought did fleetingly cross my mind on that occasion.

The trouble was with those guys, they were not that sensitive about their horses and they got one of them out into the yard and then scared it by shooing it and waving a stick at it. They weren't hurting it, they just wanted it to rush about in a panic so that they could see how beautiful it was. I told them off and told them they should be more considerate, loving and sensitive to animals. They found that amusing and just laughed at me.

The 3 of us set off to visit the horse in the mountains. Miguel's friend offered the English lady some silly amount of money, which she turned down. He was obviously a dealer and she would never know what would happen to her horse. I heard later that she sold it to an English family in some neighbouring village who already had about 4 horses, that way she knew where it was going. I had met this family because they occasionally rode through our village, and we had stopped to chat and have a drink in the bar. They offered holidays where people could ride. They were very nice people and I was happy about the outcome.

Lots of Work

In the meantime, work was going well. Quite a few clients were coming to see me, some driving as many as 40 or 50 miles. The first Alternative Medicine Exhibition opened on the coast near Marbella, and I was offered a stand there. It lasted 3 days and I stayed overnight with friends. It was very well attended, and we had a lecture room where some of us were invited to give talks. I gave talks on various aspects of my work. The lectures needed to be in English, French and Spanish. It was all very well organised and advertised. A few of us went out on different radio stations beforehand to talk about our work, which was all very exciting. I was also pleased to do some live translations, at the actual venue, translating various interviews into Spanish for the local radio stations. This was the beginning of quite a lot of these Alternative Medicine exhibitions, and details of the treatments are described in my book Divine Communication and also a third book I am writing.

I also worked giving treatments at the Vegetarian Society in Malaga. The owner was an interesting man who lived near me. He cared passionately about the under-privileged and had recently been on a hunger strike for a few days in protest over the treatment of gypsies in Mijas. In an attempt to 'clean up' the village to attract the tourists and keep the foreigners happy, the local authorities had blatantly bulldozed down a large settlement of shacks belonging to the gypsies on the outskirts, destroying every home. Dozens of people with children were then left to sleep in the open with no shelter, lying on the soil surrounded by rubbish and trying to survive in all weathers.

Pamela Having Fun

Pamela was now a beautiful girl and was trying to fend off endless attention from local boys. She seemed to be getting friendly with all sorts of young people and started going to the coast on Saturday night until very late. I would pick up a crowd of young girls from various villages—I had a Nissan Patrol 4 wheel drive by this time—and drop them all off and then put my alarm on for about 2 or 3 am and get up and collect them all. Other parents also took their turns. The whole town would be jumping until 7 a.m., every bar and club open all night, streets full of youngsters. At college, she had met a delightful young man and they went out for quite a while. My phone bill around that time was astronomical and I couldn't understand it, as Pamela swore it wasn't her using it. Unfortunately for her, we were in the first area in the whole country where we suddenly received an itemised bill, and there for all to see on the bill were 65 phone calls to her boyfriend in one month.

Then, at the age of 14, she asked me if she could go to Madrid for the weekend to see U2 with a bunch of friends from college. There were about 6 of them, including her boyfriend Alvaro. She seemed incredibly young for such a drama but the inevitable pressure caved me in, and I did like her boyfriend. He seemed delightful, his parents were teachers, and so I said she could go.

Once again, my neighbours said I had taken leave of my senses, and I was inclined to agree with them. She left on a Friday night by train and got home Monday morning, by which time I was a nervous wreck. We didn't have mobile phones at that time. As I met her from a bus down at the coast and I saw her walking towards me, I was so utterly relieved I thought I would never let her out of my sight again.

I had heard the tale of a friend of hers at college who was crazy about The Cure. She and her friend, both aged 14, begged their mothers to let them go to Madrid to see them in concert. Spanish mothers on the whole are very strict, especially so in the villages, and they were absolutely forbidden. They then each told their parents that they were staying the weekend with the other one, went to Malaga airport, caught a plane to Madrid and went to see the concert. The mothers didn't find out for 6 months when one of them discovered the tickets in a bedroom drawer.

Pamela and I often went away for the weekend to stay with our lovely Danish friend. We had met the first time I had gone to Fuengirola and we had been firm friends ever since. She had a delightful villa with a swimming pool and we all went out for meals and trips to the beach and markets. Her villa had been robbed twice and a lot of very valuable jewellery had been stolen, including family heirlooms. The thieves had actually prised the rejas right out of the walls with a crowbar. Rejas are several bars of heavy metal welded together in an artistic way, painted black and actually cemented into the walls for the very purpose of keeping the property safe. All houses had them and they were often fitted over the main doors also.

One of our favourite outings was to the Fuengirola market, actually situated at the time in nearby Los Boliches, an enormous street market with hundreds of stalls selling everything imaginable—fantastic arrays of fruits and vegetables, local earthenware pottery, books, antiques, paintings and clothes. The colour and vibrancy of the market, full of gypsies and Moroccans, was intoxicating. It was by far the best market in southern Andalucía, and people travelled from great distances to sell wares and to visit.

Along Comes Geraldo

I was still renting rooms and one day a man arrived from Malaga, looking for a room to live for some time. He looked at the room I offered him and seemed very pleased with it. He said he would take it. He left me some money and said he would only use it at weekends to start with. He did, however, pay me for the whole week. He had 2 small children; one was 2, the other 9 months. He had separated from his partner. He had a business in Malaga, and after a while he moved in permanently. He was quiet and gentle, well-mannered and sensitive, and we were very pleased.

He had been living in our house for about 3 months when one of my dearest friends Sylvia arrived to stay from Switzerland. We had met when we were 17; we had both started working for the Swiss Bank in London the same week, although Sylvia had started 2 days after me because she had been playing violin in a concert in the Festival Hall. She was really taken with Geraldo and jokingly asked me to translate an offer to return to Switzerland with her! She then asked me why I wasn't interested in the man romantically, and in surprise, I said I hadn't really noticed him. She pointed out that he took great care of his children, cooked wonderful meals and seemed altogether very pleasant. I had been lonely for a long time, but still he hadn't registered.

After her comments, I began to be more aware of him and we spent many evenings talking and exchanging our life stories. He had 2 other grown up children in their twenties from a previous marriage, and then I discovered he was actually going out with a 17-year-old! He began to look rather scary and I decided he wasn't a good idea. However, he told me more than once that he wasn't interested in the young girl and was looking for a woman more his age.

His presence in the house certainly improved my Spanish, as we seemed to be talking non-stop every evening when he got in from work. He didn't ever correct me, although I often wished that he would. He said he didn't like to and thought it would discourage me. His son would do so, however, and was quite intolerant if I made even the smallest mistake, telling me that it just wasn't good enough, that I should be speaking perfectly. I did find this rather disheartening.

Then one afternoon, I went to collect Tammy from where I had tethered her in the morning and she was gone. The long rope she had been tethered to was also missing, so I guessed that it had come loose and she was around somewhere. I searched everywhere and became more and more frantic as time went on. By the time Geraldo came home from work, I was almost hysterical. It was quite late when he arrived, about 9 p.m. When I told him what had happened, he insisted on going straight out to look for her. We jumped into his 4 wheel drive and he drove through river beds, over hills and banks in the pitch dark, searching everywhere. We were gone for hours, and didn't find her. He hadn't even had a drink or eaten. We went home and I was very despondent. I couldn't sleep. At 7 a.m. the next day, driving my daughter to the next village where she caught the school bus, I saw Tammy slowly coming out of the scrub, looking very happy and very full with the huge length of rope trailing behind her. The relief I felt was immense.

However, the incident had changed the way I felt about that man, and now I saw him quite differently. I was very impressed by the way he had tried to find her, and I think we became closer friends after that. It probably wasn't long after that when our relationship began. We were very happy together and it was nice to have a family around again and it was good for Pamela too. His children were sweet and we enjoyed a lot of fun at the weekends, having picnics along river beds in remote spots. Gerardo and I went out over the hills on his motorbike, which was great fun, riding up hairy tracks and often falling off. His other two children would come and stay from Barcelona and we all had some very enjoyable times together.

Unfortunately for me, very soon after he moved in, he had seen a cottage on the outskirts of the village which was empty and had made enquiries and taken it. I heard about it from the owner before he had a chance to tell me. It turned out to be a delight, as it had several acres of land and fruit trees, and we were able to have privacy away from the neighbours. We all enjoyed the cottage very much and had big family get-togethers there with barbecues and meals. It was extra grazing for Tammy too, so she used to come also for the day, together with the dog, who had a great time. After a few months, Geraldo actually moved back in with me but continued to keep the cottage. It was his bolt hole. He was very commitment-phobic and he needed it. With his history, I was pretty nervous of him too.

Pots Galore

I had been struggling for a couple of years to get my new gas kiln working and had been frequently visiting Pepita, my potter friend in the village, talking to her, looking at her kiln and trying to understand how to work it out. She came to look at mine and other friends tried to help, but nobody was sure how to do it. I had known her for years. Since the day we had purchased the house, a neighbour, hearing that I made pots, took me to see her.

She astonished me one day when I was talking to her about my kiln and I had momentarily forgotten the word for burner, quemador. She suddenly said the word in English. To know the word burner in English seemed very impressive! I was amazed to discover that she spoke excellent English, having lived in London for some years, but she had never told me. She was a member of the opposition party at the town hall and had been struggling against the corruption for a long time and became a great ally to us in our later battle.

She is married to a well-known artist who paints and exhibits extraordinary and outlandish pictures that are very Dalí-like.

She recommended a guy to come and help me, he had installed her kiln satisfactorily, but trying to translate the technicalities of the English manual and explain to him how to do it when I barely understood it myself was too much for both of us. He had a mental block that he couldn't do it because the kiln was English. I tried to explain to him that it would work just the same as Pepita's, but he wouldn't have it. It was very frustrating, having it standing there and not using it. Then one day, I was talking to an Australian friend in my healing group in Fuengirola, and he offered to come and help me. He spent the day welding copper tubes and installing the kiln, which was to be fired with propane gas, only to find at the end of the day that one of the two burners wouldn't work. He had run out of time, but I was very grateful to him and felt that we were nearly there. A few people looked at the burner and tried to fix it, but with no luck.

Explaining this to Geraldo, he took the burner to pieces and found an insect nest had been blocking it and at last, I had it up and running. Pepita had told me where to buy materials in Malaga some months before, and I had taken over a bedroom in the house and turned it into my studio. I had stacks of stoneware pots made and ready to fire. The first time we fired it was terrifying. In fact, I would say every time we fired it was terrifying. The kiln room was next door to the stable, so we had to move Tammy out onto land furthest away to be safe. The burners roared loudly, the gas bottles kept freezing over and we constantly had to hose them down. After having an electric kiln for as long as I could remember, this was a whole new experience, which I found very unnerving. In addition, I felt that if anything was to go wrong with the heat, I was going to lose an awful lot of pots, as it was a much bigger kiln than my electric and it was stacked full with a variety of pots, including teapots, bowls, jugs and sculptures.

I read and reread the instructions on stacking and firing, up draughts and down draughts, circulation of heat and reduction firing and translated it all for Geraldo, who grasped it all very quickly and certainly understood it better than I did. The first time we lit the burners and began firing, we spent the entire night up in the garden, pacing back and forth, watching it, monitoring it and hosing down the bottles. Firing a kiln can take anything up to 12 hours or more. The noise of the burners and all the commotion brought out the neighbours and we reassured them that we would try very hard not to blow anything up. It all went very well and for me, it was intensely exciting to be producing pottery again. It was even more nerve racking, however, when we fired the kiln full of glazed pottery, because this was so uncertain. The temperatures had to be so much higher, therefore the kiln was on for so much longer. It did all turn out very well, in any case.

This enabled me to begin exhibiting and selling. I joined an art group on the coast, a mixed group of eccentric people, managed by Manolo, a very pleasant and reasonable man. We regularly met in a hotel to discuss how to sell our wares. Manolo got permission from the town hall for us to have a street market on Sunday mornings, right on the sea front. It was a beautiful spot, with lovely sands and views of the sea. It was a perfect place where people strolled or walked their dogs. Youngsters would come along on their skate boards and others would be having drinks on outside tables in the sun. Doing markets selling arts and crafts involved some effort, packing tables and chairs, boxing up the pots, getting it all laid out, but this location was so wonderful, it was an utter joy to be there. In addition, there were about a dozen of us with tables and it was a very pleasant social occasion. There were paintings, jewellery and other craft work. Passers-by were interested and we all sold some of our wares.

One family was quite fascinating, a mixture of mainly Irish and Asian, they lived in a caravan in a lay-by up in the mountains, where they were making and selling their jewellery. They were all very interesting and one of their sons was studying at university, spoke several languages and was extremely good looking and about the same age as Pamela. I needed a useful incentive to get her to come and help me on a Sunday morning when all she wanted to do was stay in bed. She refused at first, saying she was sure he wouldn't be at all interesting and I wouldn't have any idea of the kind of boy she'd like. However, once she met him, she became quite smitten and they made friends and went out together for a while.

Unfortunately, one Sunday morning after we had been going for a few weeks, the police arrived, told us we had no right to be there and moved us all on. Manolo explained that we had a permit from the town hall, but they wouldn't listen. Local people got to know I was selling pots but some people almost collapsed at my prices, used as they were to really cheap earthenware pots in the markets.

Ricardo

Ricardo was a well-known artist in the village. We met him when Pamela won a painting competition and he presented her with a prize. We had a lot of interesting times in his home. He and his partner, Jose, a doctor, threw a lot of parties. People arrived from all over the country, some of them fascinating characters and all different nationalities. Jose actually got married just before we met him, which had evidently caused quite a scandal, as well as an upset to his partner, as his wife knew he was gay before she married him but still they went ahead. It lasted for a couple of years whilst he had affairs with other men and she eventually left him and went to live in Madrid with someone else.

I also did a lot of healings in that house for Ricardo when he was seriously ill with bowel cancer, and I was often called out to many of his friends. A couple of his friends had AIDS. After he became very ill, he had his well water analysed and discovered that it was 97% contaminated with faeces. The village sewers were draining into nearby land and seeping into his well. He was naturally horrified and kicked up an almighty fuss with the town hall. The mayor, being who he was, refused to cooperate and after a couple of years of struggling and fighting, Ricardo took the town hall to court. In the meantime, everybody rallied round and took him bottles of the local spring water.

A Wonderful Art/Pottery Weekend

He and I decided to join forces and run an art/pottery weekend. We advertised and sent out lots of fliers to people we thought may be interested and got a great response. We had about 8 participants and agreed to have them sleep at my house as I had lots of bedrooms, Geraldo, who was an excellent cook, would do the cooking, and then in the mornings, those who wanted would make pottery with me in my studio and in the afternoons do some painting at Ricardo's house. This was very successful, apart from one of the women breaking my kick wheel whilst trying to constantly spin it in the wrong direction. Geraldo thankfully welded it back together for me. It was romantically fruitful in that two of the people on the course got together and have been partners ever since.

An Exhibition

Ricardo one day invited me to exhibit my pottery, and we held the exhibition of my work and his paintings in his house, which was very unusual and beautiful with great character, very old wooden doors painted with crazy characters like Don Quijote and lovely antique furniture. My pottery was displayed in every room and Ricardo's paintings were hung already on every bit of wall space. The house filled with people, many of them had travelled great distances to attend and Pamela and a friend of hers volunteered to serve drinks for everybody. We ended the exhibition with a grand sit down feast and about 25 guests.

I met a delightful potter/sculptor who worked in Malaga and had a shop on the coast. He invited me to take some pieces of sculpture and put them up for sale. In summer, during the feria, I was also invited to participate in a further exhibition together with all the artists in the village. Also, several boxes of my pots went up to Barcelona to a shop and so one way and another, my pots were getting around, and that made me very happy.

Off Backpacking to China

My son had been ringing me from Hong Kong, constantly asking me to go and see him and go backpacking from there with him to wherever I fancied. I, in turn, constantly kept saying it was impossible for me to get away. However, one day whilst lying in the dentist chair with my mouth clamped open, I finally decided I desperately wanted to go. With Geraldo able to take care of Pamela and the animals, I made the arrangements. I had longed to go to Hong Kong for as long as I could remember. Will told me to choose anywhere I pleased to go travelling, as he was giving up his flat and leaving Hong Kong to spend another couple of years backpacking.

China was a place I had always dreamt of going. So, with a borrowed backpack containing a sleeping bag and a spare pair of knickers and wearing Pamela's Doc Martin boots, which I had had to practise walking in as I hadn't even been able to lift my feet up off the floor when I first put them on, they were so heavy, I set off. We spent a fabulous week together in Hong Kong, then Will packed up piles of his stuff and shipped it all home, said goodbye to Susan, his sweet, beautiful Chinese girlfriend who was in floods of tears, and off we went on the train north to the border, got out, walked through customs and there we were in the streets of China, free as birds.

We jumped on trains and buses all over the country, wild journeys into the middle of nowhere. In Canton bus station, I tried to do a pee and paid an old man sitting on a chair what I worked out later to be the equivalent of an eighth of a farthing, though I actually gave him about 25pence, which he handed back to me in horror. I then proceeded down some dark, squelching, slippery stone steps covered in black slime to a filthy communal lavatory awash and swilling in stinking brown liquid which lapped round my boots. The open room had several holes in the floor and heading for one hole and trying not to breathe in the putrid stench, I proceeded to pull down my trousers and got ready to bend down and do a pee over the hole, when half a dozen women scurried over and crouched down staring at my private parts, causing my bladder to seize up in shock. Unable to function, all my bodily outgoings went on strike thereafter and showed not a flicker of desire to disgorge a thing for the following 18 hours.

We eventually got on a small old creaking ramshackle bus piled high with luggage inside and outside on top of the roof and spent 18 hours lurching across waterlogged land to get to Yangshuo. It was mile upon mile of nothing but haunting expanses of water, mist and willow trees in every direction. We were travelling on what seemed to be a mud path between endless lakes and swamps, where the odd bus had swerved off the path and was half submerged in the water with or without its inhabitants. Not wanting to miss a single detail of this amazing journey, I refused to sleep. When the bus stopped, we had to climb out of the window to do a pee, or crawl along on our hands and knees on top of the luggage piled high in the aisle to get out. When my bladder finally decided it needed to empty itself, it took one look at what appeared to be public toilets and only agreed to function behind a bush.

Will's ability to speak Cantonese had got us to Canton alright, but thereafter nobody could understand it and the only language spoken was Mandarin. The journey was supposed to have lasted 14 hours, so when we didn't reach our destination in that time, Will got depressed, thinking we had actually got on the wrong bus and we couldn't get anyone to understand where we wanted to go. Finally, after 18 hours, the most spectacular views it is possible to behold appeared before us and we were overjoyed to know that we were where we were trying to be— Yangshuo. It was a small town on the river Li Jiang amidst such stunning scenery that we were enraptured. I was beside myself with excitement. Huge heavenly rocky sculptured karsts rose up and out of the ground and river in delightful surreal shapes shrouded in mist. It was as though we had arrived in a different world, one which the wildest imagination could never have mustered.

The food we ate in this village was out of this world, but after one simply divine 3-course meal in a pretty fairly clean café, which cost us a total of £3 for the 2 of us, I asked to go to the toilet. I was then led through the kitchens, the walls of which were covered in wet black running slime, the worktop and sink the same colour, and the toilet was a hole in the ground at the end of the kitchen covered by a disgustingly dirty curtain. Suddenly, the meal hadn't tasted as good as I thought.

After a few days there, we set off on a journey of 8 hours down the Li Jiang River in a small boat and were dropped off by the edge of the water onto a tiny beach, where I balanced my backpack on a rock, now much heavier, I having bought up half the local market. I hoisted it on to my back and trying to look brave for my son's sake, gazed at the steep dense jungle undergrowth growing right down to the water's edge. I silently, fearfully and fervently prayed for the apparition of a tour guide with a set of keys to a luxury coach he had parked round the corner. My prayers unanswered, we set off clambering upwards through the bushes and trees whilst I desperately tried not to think of tigers, snakes and spiders. After some while, we came across a man cutting some wood who stared at us appearing through some scrub, thinking he was having a vision, until at the top of the climb, we eventually arrived at a few shacks in a clearing. The people around rushed at us, touching our hair and noses, staring as though we had landed from outer space.

Amongst our other adventures, we were thrown off a bus out in the wilderness somewhere because Will refused to pay the tourist rate, which was much higher than the local rate. Then after spending 36 hours on a train to Beijing, we were arrested in Beijing station because we had the wrong tickets, and our passports were taken from us. We had been ripped off, having paid full price for the tourist tickets, we were unknowingly given tickets for locals. I managed to find someone who could translate and when he appeared to get nowhere, I had hysterics but finally, our passports were returned to us and we could continue our journey. We hiked along the Great Wall, visited palaces of all sorts, did markets and walked miles round the strange and tatty streets of the capital city, dodging bicycles at every turn.

After three weeks, our time together was up and I had to fly back to Hong Kong and then back to Madrid and Malaga, leaving my son to get himself to Mongolia, which we had gazed at from the Wall. Never had I felt as utterly restless, caged and trapped as when I returned home and was faced again with the school run, the breakfasts, teaching classes, feeding animals, cooking, washing and cleaning. I paced the length of my sitting room, my whole being longing and screaming out to be back travelling with my son in Mongolia. I was hysterical. It took me three full weeks to calm down.

Alcoholics Anonymous

Geraldo had come to the village because he and a business partner were planning to build a centre for alcoholics. They had already had discussions with the town hall regarding the available land. He talked at length about his plans and it looked as though there could be an opening for me as a therapist/counsellor. As I had no experience with alcoholics, we both took ourselves off to the centre in Malaga, the equivalent of AA, and asked their permission to join in the weekly sessions, in order to study and learn. Geraldo's father had been an alcoholic and his childhood had been very difficult. He also joined a regular class for sons and daughters of alcoholics.

Those weekly sessions were a revelation to me. At first, I had difficulty in following the language. We attended these classes for 9 months and the sessions were traumatic and moving, and I invariably ended up in tears. It astounded me to hear what family members of alcoholics had to go through—and often for many years. The sessions are conducted in order to help all family members to cope, not just the alcoholic person.

One couple who helped to run the sessions usually told their story every week, as there were always newcomers arriving. Jose had been an alcoholic for 20 years and his wife and sons often had to pick him up from the street and carry him home. He caused the most horrendous scenes and his family had a terrible life. One day, after 20 nightmare years of verbal and physical abuse, his wife decided she couldn't take it anymore and left. Jose was so devastated that he stopped drinking immediately. They finally got back together and when I met them, he had fortunately been sober for many years. We were invited to a couple's wedding in the group—alcohol free, of course.

As a result of Geraldo's childhood, he was paranoid about drinking and did not want me to drink anything at all, not even a glass of wine. I found this very difficult, especially as I loved the sweet raisin wine, vino dulce. Some local friends made it and sold it from their home. Whenever I visited them, I took two or three empty bottles and had them filled. My assurance that I would not become alcoholic had no effect on him whatsoever. He had somehow acquired a barrel of vino dulce, which he kept for visitors and kept it locked in his cottage. I was only allowed a tiny drop on rare occasions.

However, one day, his cottage was robbed and almost everything he owned was taken, including some of my things. They smashed his front door in. I was alerted by a neighbour. It was a shocking sight. They had tipped all his wine out of the barrel all over the floor and then dumped unwanted clothes and papers in it and taken the barrel. A couple of weeks later, he was driving my Seat Panda down to his cottage on a narrow dirt track when he met a van coming up and instinctually knew that it was the same guy who had robbed him before. He proceeded to try and ram him. The guy somehow half drove over the edge of the track, hit my car and came to a halt. They both jumped out and Geraldo chased the guy over the hills but couldn't catch him.

Down to Serious Business

We soon got down to some serious business. I had been telling him about the mayor persecuting me and trying to steal my land, and he was utterly outraged. He took up my case as though he was my lawyer and embarked on the massive task of not only fighting for my case but unearthing every bit of corruption the town hall was involved in—and there was a great deal. He was very well equipped; he was trained in law and had a bookshop selling law books to lawyers. There was very little he didn't know about the law and he had every detail of the law at his disposal. He was a fighter and a great defender of the downtrodden. He was heaven sent.

He had done some fantastic work for Africa years before in Barcelona. He had set up an organisation with voluntary helpers where he rented a huge warehouse. Food, unwanted clothes and goods were brought there and packed up and sent by ship to those in need in Africa. He also began a system in Barcelona where everybody took unwanted medicines back to their chemists and these were all collected and also shipped out to Africa. This system is still operating in the city to-day. He had also been involved in the anti-Franco demonstrations in his youth in the streets and been beaten over the head many times for his efforts by Franco's henchmen. He wasn't very big, in fact, he was quite slight, but he wasn't afraid of anybody or anything.

An Utterly Corrupt Mayor

Our whole village was quite terrified of the mayor and his family. There was nobody there who had the courage to stand up to them. There were tremendous undercurrents of hatred amongst the people, which stemmed from the time of Franco, and Geraldo had various meetings with a gentleman down in the river bed amongst the cane plants, so that nobody would see them talking. This man told him about how the village was divided. Certain families hated each other and with good reason. Franco's men had had 60 people murdered in and around the village because they were against him, and he told us it was the mayor's father who had arranged these assassinations. So many families had lost relatives in this way, and the people would never forget or forgive.

Even though that had been a long time ago, that was a lot of assassinations in such a small village. There was evidently a list of people to be murdered and this gentleman telling us had been on that list. For some reason, the vendetta had been finally called off and the man had therefore escaped the death sentence. His daughter, however, had married into the mayor's family and therefore had complicated matters.

It seemed that the power of this family was still strangling the village. To us, it seemed astonishing that in that day and age, the mayor could be getting away with such obvious corruption under everybody's noses. It seemed everybody knew about it but were too scared to do anything about it. The family were getting perks and a lot of other people were suffering, some of them very badly.

Some families had been driven from the village by threats and their houses stolen. We interviewed those we could track down. A lot of people were delighted that we had begun our fight back on behalf of the people but were too frightened to say so and some were too afraid to talk to us even after the battle began.

The Battle Commences

Geraldo began working full time on his computer for months on end, compiling masses of information. His bookshop was being managed by staff. One or two of the opposition members in the local town hall supplied him with documents and details. He had a formidable pile of papers and information about all sorts of dodgy deals which had lined the pockets of the mayor and his assistant and other members of his party at the town hall.

There were constant threats to people if anybody brought attention to these illegal activities. The leader of the opposition party had recently built a beautiful house on a piece of land for himself and his family. He threatened to go the newspapers with some of the corruption that was occurring but was told that if he brought these scandals into the open, the town hall would snatch his house because it had been built on town hall land and had never been legal. This was totally untrue, but the mayor seemed to think he could make anything stick. Another member of the opposition was trying to buy a plot of land to build an art gallery. There was a huge fuss, lawyers were called in by the mayor to try everything in his power to prevent it, simply because he wanted the land. The mayor used lawyers the whole time to undermine everybody, because he didn't have to foot the bill, the town hall did. His female secretary was involved in the scams. They had voted in her salary and she was earning the same amount of money as a secretary working in a town hall in Madrid. This kept her mouth shut.

We Print a Magazine

Then Geraldo began publishing a magazine in which he drew cartoons of the guilty parties. The first edition showed the mayor leaving the town hall with a big swag of cash in a bag. He put in captions and indicated very clearly that he knew exactly what was going on with various deals they had made between them. He accused him outright of being a thief, a liar and a cheat and then drew cartoons of him behind bars. He used outrageous language and swearwords.

The first magazine was printed and Sandra was staying with us at that time. She and Geraldo walked the streets distributing one to each house, to about 350 people in all. When they had finished, the streets were utterly bare and not a soul was seen for several hours. We, however, received a telephone call threatening to kill us if we didn't stop this campaign immediately. The next morning, the mayor and about 4 of his henchmen arrived at my house and told me that I could fence my land, and build whatever I would like there, including another house if I wanted. We told them all to piss off. Blackmail wasn't an option, and though I desperately wanted to fence my land, by this time, we wanted to continue exposing these disgraceful people. Our aim was to not only get the mayor out of power but to also put him in jail. We were on a mission.

Josefina and Pepe

One family in particular had suffered appallingly. They had been running a thriving restaurant with nice home-cooked food, we had eaten there years earlier. They also supplied the village with gas bottles. The lorry came to the village and unloaded dozens of bottles into their garden and the people then bought from them. Then the mayor's brother wanted to open a restaurant of his own. So the mayor and his cronies marched into the restaurant, literally kicked out the family, a couple with three children, into the street, and closed it down.

The house and business had been left to the woman by her uncle. There was a clear will to say so, but they hadn't got the money or education to fight legally and were forced to go and live nearby with an aged aunt. Some kind of legal action was supposed to have begun but nothing ever happened. The mayor, as usual, seemed to think it belonged to him. They had lost not only their home but their livelihood as well. They hadn't even been given enough time to gather all their belongings. All their beautiful plants inside and outside in the gardens had been left behind and all died.

I felt as outraged about this as Geraldo did, and we tried to do everything to help this family. They had been forced to open up their aunt's back kitchen door and try and sell a few drinks from their step in order to survive. Unfortunately, they were too scared of losing even this meagre existence to do anything about it. We were preparing endless amounts of denuncias at this time. A denuncia is like a writ, which you issue at the courts or at the police station against somebody. In this case, the denuncias were all being prepared against the mayor and his associates. We wanted to denounce that particular act of illegal treachery but needed the couple's co-operation and signatures. We tried to persuade them many times, but they were almost too scared to talk to us.

The Swedish Gentleman

Some years earlier, before we had bought our house in the village, a Swedish man had been given a piece of land there. There was a scheme going on, whereby land was given free to encourage people to go and live there. He then commuted from Sweden and built his house, much like we had done, slowly and over a period of time. When he had completed the project and made himself a beautiful dwelling, the mayor and his wife moved in. The next time the poor man came to the village to stay in his house, he had a terrible shock. He called a lawyer who came to the village; there was much shouting and arguing evidently but all to no avail. Once again, the mayor had his way and somehow got away with it. We got in touch with the Swedish embassy and did our best to find that man.

Unpleasant Scenes

It made me extremely angry when I heard about that case and made me more determined than ever to keep fighting along with Geraldo. He and I created some unbelievable scenes. In general, the situation had become extremely tense around us and I was pretty nervous. Neighbours related to the mayor who had previously been very friendly became hostile. Many stopped speaking to us. Pamela was shunned by their children and even thrown out of the bar one day when she was with her friends, the bar being owned by the mayor's brother.

I was spat on a few times until one day, I had Pamela's boyfriend with me, a big 6ft bloke and we went after the culprit, a young man about 22 who had often been in my house and we had got on very well with him. I told him firmly that his behaviour was unacceptable and that I had done nothing to deserve it, I was simply fighting for the justice of a lot of people who had suffered in the village. His mother, however, was the sister of the mayor's right hand man in the town hall. I furthermore told him straight that if he ever did it again, this man with me would beat him to a pulp. It doesn't sound very nice to threaten violence but we needed to assert ourselves, it wasn't very nice being spat on and it certainly worked. The young man never did it again.

All the while these events were taking place, I was constantly re-applying to fence my land and it was being constantly turned down. The public were allowed to go to town hall meetings and listen. Sometimes, Geraldo took his video camera and set it up beforehand. Other times, we called the press who brought a photographer. So, as the meeting was about to begin, we would burst in with video camera, press and photographer and make a huge commotion and disrupt the proceedings as much as possible. With the press listening and the cameras rolling, the mayor had to be very careful what he said. Geraldo would then interrupt with piles of papers regarding legalities, not only about my case but about other people's. Sometimes they tried to bar Geraldo from taking in the video camera, but he kicked up such a fuss and shouted and hurled abuse to such an extent that in order for the meeting to proceed, they had to give in. It was all very nerve-racking.

On one occasion, with the press and photographer there and the video rolling, I tackled the mayor and other members of the town hall about my land and started getting very angry. I then launched into the sorry tale about how the mayor had stolen his house from the Swedish man who had built it and was really shouting my head off. It seems I was also waving my fist. I shouted out that we had tracked down the man and he was going to take the mayor to court with our assistance. The photograph of me yelling at the mayor with my arm raised with a clenched fist went into several major national newspapers. One main national broad sheet paper carried an entire half page photograph of this exchange.

By this time and with articles going out in the press about all the scandals, the mayor and his cronies were getting very nervous. We were talking about getting them all put in jail. They started trying to back-pedal one or two of the deals but there was no stopping us. We had so many more cases of corruption under investigation with more and more proof as the weeks went by. One member of the town hall quit because he was too scared to continue. The secretary suddenly disappeared.

Even though we were gaining momentum, some of the people who were really on our side were still too afraid to openly talk to us or be seen with us. A few congratulated us when there was nobody about and told us to keep going, that we were doing a great job.

A Ghastly Event

Geraldo, in the meantime, decided to confront the mayor directly by building a fence around my property anyway, without permission. They had turned down our applications so many times and out of sheer bloody-mindedness. We had made some beautiful drawings, to scale with every possible detail, legal in every aspect and with all correct measurements. I wasn't keen on the idea of building without permission, but Geraldo was adamant. He dug lots of large holes all-round the perimeter and sank fence poles into a concrete base. The mayor lived at the top of the hill and could see what was going on. I found it amusing to watch the mayor standing at the top of the hill glaring down at Geraldo and Geraldo at the bottom of the hill leaning on his spade, glaring back up, like two cocks getting ready for a fight. And a hell of a fight was what we ended up with. After a few days, the mayor marched down the hill with an official-looking gentleman who approached me and handed me papers from the courts, ordering me to stop work, by law, as what we were doing was illegal. I had to sign the papers.

I was naturally getting scared and asked Geraldo to stop work. Not a chance, he wasn't having any of it and insisted on carrying on regardless. That was all very well, I admired his stance but the property was in my name, and I was beginning to wonder if I might end up in a Spanish jail, with the way things were going. A few more days passed, and he had more or less completed the fence when matters took a dreadful turn for the worse.

It was about 3 p.m. when I heard the most horrendous commotion going on outside. I opened my front door to see a huge crowd of people marching towards the house. The mayor, full of himself as usual and smiling broadly, was leading 4 policemen and a huge digger, with about 50 people following. I approached them and asked them what the hell was going on. The policemen informed me that they were going to bulldoze down my fence as it was illegal, and if I didn't want my car to be wrecked, would I move it? I was about to leave the house to go and collect Pamela from the next village where I met the school bus. Geraldo was at that time doing some work on his cottage about a mile away and I hastily got in the car, made sure the horse and animals were safely away, drove like mad down to his house and told him what was going on and to get home as quickly as possible. I then dashed off and picked up Pamela.

By the time I got back, Geraldo had arrived and set up his video camera on a tripod in the garden to film the whole proceedings. It was like something out of medieval times, a jeering mob shouting and swearing at Geraldo, lots of children included. They were calling him every name under the sun, their favourite insult being that your mother is a prostitute. I went out and surveyed the whole scene. I noted who was there and who wasn't and I noticed some people looking at me very sheepishly, a few couldn't look at me at all. I had got on very well with everybody in the village before all this had blown up, and I knew almost everybody very well, especially the children. I was pleased to notice that many of the children were embarrassed with me there.

The big enemy for them was Geraldo, and they did all they could to humiliate him, the police even grappled him and pushed him around very harshly, even pushing him down to the ground, when he stood just inside the fence on my land to try and prevent the bulldozer from destroying all his work. A few of the men took the opportunity to push him about also and I screamed at everybody, including the police to leave him alone, that they had no right to physically abuse him as he was standing on my land. I threatened to denounce everybody in sight, yelling that what they were all doing was totally illegal. Geraldo shouted instructions to me about the video camera, where to position it, and I made sure I got all the scuffles recorded. The entire scene and all the verbal abuse was recorded perfectly.

It was all so distressing and hard to watch. I kept going indoors, leaving the video rolling, to see if Pamela was alright. It finally came to an end, the fence totally destroyed, heaps of broken wood everywhere, the concrete footings ripped up, the boundary of my land in chaos with piles of stones dislodged from the excavated bank. There were piles of rubble and concrete everywhere and all the work was undone, not only the fence destroyed but the weeks of work we had done rebuilding that part of the garden completely wrecked.

Shameful, the lot of them, the mayor, police, digger and jeering mob finally left and Geraldo walked into the house, camera equipment in hand. I was utterly relieved to see him in one piece but amazed to see his face, I had been expecting him to be forlorn and brow-beaten and instead, his face was glowing and his eyes were alight with what seemed to be triumph. He had had his cock fight with the mayor, even though we had come off worse. I was staggered that he could do this for me, try to protect me in this way, fight and suffer like this on my behalf, and I was deeply grateful. I guess he had engineered this particular battle himself against my wishes but I still felt sorry for him. He had after all come to the village to live to get out of Malaga for some peace and quiet in the mountains, but we both felt that a far greater plan beyond our control was involved here.

He couldn't wait to play back his video and listen to all that had occurred. He played and played the video over and over, listened to every word and we both saw in detail who was there, what they said and how they behaved. Copies of the video were made and one later went to the Court House as part of all the mass of evidence we presented with all the cases of corruption against the mayor and his associates.

This horrendous day wasn't over, however. A few hours later at 2.30 a.m., I suffered a severe asthma attack from the shock of it all and Geraldo had to rush me to the emergency department of the hospital for treatment. He made sure the hospital authorities knew exactly what had caused it

Not long after this, the mayor decided to denounce me for trying to take 'his' land and he took me to court and lost. My lawyer successfully defended me and with all my papers in perfect order, the mayor really had not had a leg to stand on. He still would not however accept that the land was mine out of sheer bloody-mindedness or allow me to fence it. This man took no notice of the law. He could sue anybody for anything at any time because it cost him nothing. He used public funds and employed lawyers to do his bidding. That was the power of mayors in Spain. I was not going to give up the fight to protect my land from that thief and by that time, we were hell bent on bringing him down.

Endless Dramas

Tensions were running high, especially as we were surrounded with the mayor's sisters and brothers and one day some neighbours arrived, walking straight into my garden uninvited, spoiling for a fight, accusing one of Geraldo' dogs of killing one of their chickens. As I knew nothing about it, hadn't seen the incident and didn't believe it, I asked them politely to get off my land. They then got nasty, started screaming abuse and shouting the same old song that the land wasn't mine. One of them picked up a huge rock and raised it over his head and threatened to kill me with it. As I was directly below him on a lower piece of ground, it was very unnerving. I managed to say that they would very much regret this incident and I told them to get out, they left with disgusting foul language and threats spilling out of their mouths.

When I told Geraldo about it, he urged me to denounce them, as this was totally unacceptable and all part of the mayor and his family's intimidation of us, trying as they had done so many times before to get us to cave in. Once again, I was back in court, a writ against them for threatening to kill me. Once again, my lawyer won the case and my neighbours were fined and given a suspended prison sentence. As they left the court house, they screamed such terrible abuse at all of us, my lawyer considered a further writ against them. It was a sad state of affairs and I wasn't happy about it, but we had to stay strong. So many other families had been intimidated, lost their homes and had fled. We had to keep going.

The Warehouse

One of the biggest scandals which Geraldo unearthed and documented in great detail was the sale and purchase of a huge warehouse in the village, which the town hall had built, obviously with public money allocated from town hall funds.

The mayor then sold it to his best mate, the assistant mayor, who had a building business.

The law totally prohibits dealings such as this if you are involved in the town hall.

The town hall then bought it back and so it went on, each time, both men pocketing huge sums of money. This assistant mayor, el teniente alcalde, when we first knew him, owned an old small shabby truck and used to bring up a few building materials for people. He suddenly acquired a fleet of huge trucks and was building another massive lorry compound to hold several lorries, plus an extremely large extension to his otherwise average little house. That man was given all the town hall work, which again was totally illegal. Other members of the town hall were given pieces of land to keep them quiet.

There is a legal right for anyone to ask for all town hall documents to be examined, and Geraldo asked. He examined details of dates, transactions and invoices. He talked to everybody, especially the opposition who were only too glad to cooperate, after years of struggling and frustration. Then suddenly, one night shortly afterwards, very late, people were seen leaving the town hall with huge boxes of papers and a big bonfire was taking place out the back. Many other boxes were seen being taken to houses of the mayor's relatives. In the meantime, Geraldo published all the information he had acquired in his regular news updates in his magazine, which was distributed to the population of both villages.

A lot of people everywhere were overjoyed that at last the scandal of the warehouse had been brought out in the open. They had all known about it and were outraged but felt helpless to do anything about it. Any complaints anybody made were answered by having their unemployment payments stopped and threats were made to their homes. People were terrified; it was an appalling way to have to live.

The Austrian

We had an Austrian in the village and the town hall was starting to build houses on his land. We went to see him, and he showed us his Escritura. The land was very clearly marked out—unmistakable. We begged him to back us in our fight and put in a denuncia against the mayor and town hall. He was a weak and nervous man and he refused. We visited him a couple of times, but he began to look very wary when he saw us coming. He didn't want the hassle, he only used the house for holidays and came twice a year. He was as scared as everybody else.

His land is now divided by a road and covered with several houses, built of course by members of the mayor's family who were given all the work. Building work of any description was always given to families of the mayor and his assistant. Anyone outside the families had to go to the coast and look for work.

Daylight Robbery

Geraldo tracked down one particular family and we met up with them in a hotel on the coast to hear their story. Bernardo had been a member of the same political party as the mayor but loathed the corruption he saw going on and constantly opposed and complained and threatened to report it. He had recently built a beautiful house on a very nice piece of land on the outskirts of the village. He was told, however, that unless he kept quiet about the corruption, his house and land would be seized by the town hall and they would prove that it had been built illegally. He and his family were forced to sell up and flee like everybody else. He was very bitter and angry and utterly delighted that we were doing our best to bring an end to it all. Members of the opposition party frequently complained to their political head office, but nothing was ever done to stop it.

The Doctor

We also heard about a doctor who had bought a house at the top of the village to renovate for his mother to live in. The mayor and his assistant decided they could make a lot of money out of doing up the house. They went to see him accompanied by the rest of thugs in the town hall and threatened to report him to various medical and financial authorities for all kinds of malpractice in his work, all a pack of lies, but naturally the man was terrified. They forced him to sell the house to them for an absolute song. In the meantime, the doctor's mother died. In other words, they simply robbed the house from him.

Teresa

Right opposite that house lived Teresa, an elderly lady who was a close friend of mine. I visited her often and we spent many hours chatting while I watched her crocheting. Her beautiful granddaughter and I were also good friends; she lived in Barcelona and always visited me when she came to the village. Teresa was crocheting an enormous bedspread in tiny cotton stitches, which needed the patience of a saint. I helped her with odd jobs she needed doing.

We only ever had one upset between us when she threw her cat out of her upstairs window because it was mewing for food. She didn't feed it and some other neighbours and I took it food. I didn't visit for quite a while afterwards and she wanted to know why. I told her she had badly upset me by throwing the cat out of an upstairs window and she promised she would never do it again. The poor cat was eventually poisoned, as they all are, by the illegal practice of chucking poison everywhere to kill rats.

Teresa was the sister of other close friends of mine in the next village and from all of their family, I heard many truths about what had gone on for a very long time in the village. The hatred towards the mayor and his family was palpable and hardly surprising. After the mayor and his mate had finished the renovation of the house opposite which they had so despicably obtained, it went up for sale. Every time someone came to see the house, Teresa made sure they knew the full extent of the history of the house and she successfully put everybody off. The house took about 4 years to sell. Even so, they made a huge profit. It never ceased to amaze me how those people all went to church. They and their wives would take communion, they would have their children baptised, but with a paedophile priest, what a mockery it all made of religion.

Welcome Diversions

Fortunately, amidst work and the battle, we did manage to also get out and enjoy ourselves. I had made many friends in Fuengirola by spending so much time there working. There were some pretty wild bars along the coast, and I gradually began to enjoy some of them. There were some that had very funny shows and they were a good laugh.

One evening, I was persuaded against my will to go to a bar down the coast at Los Boliches, which belonged to Ronnie Knight. He was a known criminal, once married to Barbara Windsor and wanted for his part in the £3.5 million gold bullion robbery at Heathrow airport some years before. He was regularly attacked and had his car brakes cut. My two companions introduced me to him as a psychic friend of theirs. They were regulars, and as I held his hand, I pretended to be able to read palms and turned his hand over and said I saw terrible fear written there. He whipped his hand away and said what rubbish. Perhaps that was unkind of me, but I found it utterly incongruous that he should be happily serving drinks at double the prices of anywhere else, whilst supposedly guilty of a crime for which he didn't seem to be paying.

As the evening progressed, with karaoke up and running, I was sitting between my two companions who were both gay, and they spent the evening telling me how hard it had been growing up in England, knowing that homosexuality was illegal and having threats of prison sentences hanging over them. They had been terrified. There were some very unsavoury looking characters in there, including someone they told me was a hit man, who had arrived in his flashy Mercedes with a beautiful blond by his side.

I spent the whole evening nervously watching the door, wondering if someone might burst in with a machine gun. It poignantly occurred to me how very strange my life had become and how far away my happy marriage and my former tranquil life in the fields of Somerset seemed. The last I heard, Ronnie Knight gave himself up and went to jail.

Sometime later, I was very shocked to be told that one of my companions that evening, an elderly guy with grey hair in a ponytail, in fact owned brothels both in Amsterdam and Bangkok for young boys, with whom he regularly indulged himself. This was a man who pretended to be spiritual and attended the meditation group we had running in Fuengirola with 36 participants. He was obviously using it as a respectable front. I have never been able to abide old men with grey ponytails since then. Another participant in that group was caught peddling drugs in France and ended up in jail.

A Real Surprise

One couple we made friends with had a daughter around Pamela's age, and they spent the odd weekend together in each other's homes. Her father was Paraguayan and one weekend when this young girl was staying with us, we took her with a group of friends up into the mountains inland to a beautiful forest with a wide river where people could swim and we had a picnic beneath the trees.

To get there, we had a very windy and mountainous journey of about 3 hours. On the last stretch, we had to drive along a ledge which seemed suspended in the heavens from the rocks like a mantelpiece with a sheer drop down below which seemed to go on forever. The ledge was so narrow and precarious that I got halfway along and froze with fright. I couldn't drive on and was simply paralysed in my seat. I saw my friends in cars in front disappear out of sight. My girlfriend, who was sitting next to me, had to talk to me very gently and told me not to look left and to move very carefully forward a foot at a time. We got over it to reach our destination and I spent most of the time there wondering how on earth I would drive back.

At lunch, my friends asked our young visitor about herself and then we all recalled the music phenomena of the seventies, Los Paraguayos, a fabulous group of Paraguayan musicians who were very popular in England and all over the world.

We had known the family for 18 months and had had dinner together sometimes and then I had a real surprise. On leaving their home one evening with a friend, as I was driving back to her place, she casually asked me if I knew that our Paraguayan friend was in fact the singer of the group Los Paraguayos. I had such a shock, I almost drove off the road. I could not believe it. I should have realised. He regularly serenaded our healing group, singing and playing and I had thought he was a wonderful musician, but in all that time I had never realised who he was. When I got home that evening, I rummaged through my old records and found my two long playing records of Los Paraguayos, and there he was, smiling at me from my record sleeves! I rang him and asked him why on earth he had never told me! It seemed that they wanted to keep a low profile as they had seen the spoilt behaviour of children who had well-known

118

parents and didn't want to go down that road. They hadn't even told their daughter!

We saw the late Lonnie Donegan around sometimes, the skiffle singer from the sixties; he came into my clinic one day with his wife and piles of children. Pamela found herself sitting next to him in the theatre in Fuengirola one day and they were chatting about the play we were watching. She had no idea who he was as he was around long before her time. I whispered to her in the interval that he had had a hit song called 'My Old Man's a Dustman' many moons ago. She didn't seem too impressed.

Pamela at College

Pamela was getting on extremely well at college around this time and doing the most extraordinary amount of work. For her A levels, the equivalent there was C.O.U. She was studying Latin, Ancient Greek, Spanish language, Spanish literature, French, History and Philosophy. This seemed to be an unbelievable number of subjects to be studying at A level, but it was normal in Spain. Her final year to get through entrance exams to university had us both on our knees. She was so busy and so stressed, she would be up half the night revising and sometimes the entire night. I had to test her on Latin verbs and Spanish verbs for hours on end until I nearly went crazy and could do no more. She would then continue on for several more hours.

I couldn't sleep around that time either, as I was so worried about her or would get up in the night to see if she was alright and find her surrounded by papers studying. She didn't seem to be sleeping much at all. At the time of her exams, I was constantly driving her up and down the mountain and along the coast to college for various exams at different times. I had never seen anyone so stressed or anyone work so hard, it amazed me. The pressure and strain and concern for her really got to me and there were times when I felt like I was cracking up. With the pressure of her studies and the continuing battle going on in the village, I felt like I was having a nervous breakdown. We were both immensely relieved when she passed all her exams and secured a place in Granada University.

Off to Canada

Jack's uncle in Vancouver Island kept ringing me around this time and insisting I visit him. Once again, I took the opportunity to get away, though it was winter and utterly freezing—28 degrees below at Montreal, where I had to change flights with the Lawrence River completely frozen over. The entire country was covered in snow; from the plane you saw nothing but a white carpet from east to west. I stayed in Vancouver with some dear friends who took me up to Whistler and I was astonished to see frozen lakes on the way. Although it was fractionally warmer and very pretty on Vancouver Island, I had to have 8 duvets on top of me in bed to keep warm and my uncle had to keep his heating on all day so I didn't freeze to death.

Geraldo and I Going Downhill

Despite all that we had gone through together or perhaps because of it, the relationship between Geraldo and I had started to falter. He was a nice guy, caring, loving and very brave, but he was very dominant and I found it hard to take. Although he rescued lots of animals that were abandoned, he didn't look after them very well and treated them quite badly at times. He kicked our boxer dog and screamed at him in front of my son and some friends, who were staying. They were appalled and they took me to one side and warned me they thought he was violent.

He insisted that Pamela and I talk in Spanish the whole time and never in English, which we both found absurd. He always seemed to think we were talking about him behind his back. As I was the only person talking to her regularly in English, it was essential that I continued. Apart from myself, she also spoke to my two closest friends in English, one was Italian and the other Danish. He threw tantrums when we refused, but in order to keep the peace, whenever he was around, we spoke in his language. We used to go into another room sometimes so that we could speak in our language, but he would hear us through the door and burst in and get very angry.

I cannot now believe that I ever allowed him to make us do that. It was, after all, our home.

He would also try to insist that Pamela did the housework. On this, I fought him. I told him that under no circumstances was she doing housework. She had piles of homework and studying to do, but he wouldn't relent, forever moaning at her about her responsibilities. In fact, I employed a cleaner from the village, one of the mayor's victims who badly needed the work and the money and one day, I came into the sitting room to see her rummaging through my handbag and whilst I quietly observed her, she took out my purse and tipped all the money out of it into her hand. I approached her and asked her what the hell she was doing, and she told me that she just wanted to know how much money I had. I didn't have her back.

Geraldo's two sons from Barcelona and one of their girlfriends often came to stay during their holidays. I adored them and all three of them were studying hard at college and they were very good company for Pamela. Geraldo, however, thought they should also work and have responsibilities—he had a mania about responsibilities—and had them up very early in the morning finding all kinds of jobs for them to do, picking sacks of almonds and olives at his cottage, gardening, cooking and cleaning. I would plead with him to leave them alone and let them have a holiday, some fun and a rest but he took no notice.

He also caused upsets when my own son came to stay, complaining about him and creating a huge fuss one time when he lent him his car which he then expected back sooner than Will realised. He got me to ring him and chew his ear off about it, which I greatly regretted afterwards, especially as Will was very upset about it. We did, however, have some good times and big family barbecues in the gardens and long walks over the hills with all the dogs and horse. One of his sons fell madly in love with Pamela and although she liked him, nothing serious developed between them.

He contributed nothing financially towards the running of the house whatsoever. He did buy food sometimes and often reminded me that he was like an unpaid law advisor, which was true, but I was also paying my lawyer for all the work he had to do regarding the problems affecting my land, which included several court cases.

The Mother of His Children

In addition, Carmen, the mother of his children, was forever ringing up demanding all sorts of things and he would rush off to help. She was horrid to me whenever I saw her as though their separation was my fault, even though they had parted long before I came along. She sneered at me and taunted me about the way I spoke and sarcastically asked me when I was going to learn their language. A couple of times she came after me in the street, spoiling for a fight.

Then she joined an extreme religious group. Not long afterwards, Geraldo asked me to do an allergy test on each of his children and for that I cut off a small lock of hair from each child. A couple of days later, suddenly noticing that some hair had been cut off from her children's heads, she freaked out completely, ringing up and accusing me of witchcraft. Geraldo tried to explain, but she was having none of it and refused point blank to allow him to have the children again. He then sat around the house crying about the loss of his children and begging her to change her mind.

After about 3 months, she relented on the condition that the children were not allowed to come near me. Fortunately, although Geraldo agreed in order to keep the peace, when the children arrived for weekends, he refused to abide by this condition and things soon reverted to how they had been before. In the meantime, she had her church check me out at my town hall. Fortunately, as this was before all the rumpus began with the mayor, they thankfully gave me the all clear. The whole church then started praying for me evidently, as I had obviously gone completely off the rails, food allergy testing clearly being the work of witches and the devil.

Our Relationship Ends

All of these influences and the strains of the battle in the village were all seemingly taking their toll on our relationship, and it began to sadly decline. I had never felt entirely comfortable with the relationship, as I was still grieving for my marriage. After two and half years, we separated and Geraldo returned to his cottage and eventually to the mother of his youngest children, who he had sworn he despised. After he had left, I learned some very shocking things about him which I had not known.

I still had a lot of his stuff and the next time he called one evening to collect some of it, I confronted him and we had a big bust up. The next morning when I opened my front door to get in the car to take Pamela to college and go to work, I found he had taken the car in the night. He had a spare key and had arrived in the village by taxi. This was a terrible thing to do to me without warning and I was distraught. I had to get Pamela to college and was teaching an early class at a school some 15 miles away. I had to run up the hill to my dear Italian friend and borrow her spare car. She kindly lent it to me for a few weeks until I got another one. I was very nervous about buying another car on my own, so Jack then drove us a car out from England which was a lot of effort and hassle for him, but we were extremely grateful.

Geraldo and I had swapped cars some time before, he had taken my Seat Panda as he drove to Malaga every day and it was much cheaper, and he had let me have his 4 wheel drive which suited me better for driving in between mountain villages. When we had separated, he had told me I could keep the car. This was hardly surprising, as he had not been able to make his hire purchase payments on the Nissan Patrol and after he had tried to borrow money from his parents, who refused, and his friends, who also refused, I rather reluctantly lent him £2,500 so that the company wouldn't take it away from him. In the meantime, he had driven my Panda into the ground and blown up the engine, which was beyond repair. As he had not repaid my loan, I felt I had every right to the car. He had also acquired another one.

He had gone bankrupt some years before with a previous business because he had laid off an employee due to the fact that he could no longer afford his wages. This employee, who had been a friend, took him to court and the court awarded him about £25,000. As Geraldo didn't have the money, the business which he had built up over many years folded. He was so utterly furious that he made a vow at that point to never pay the government another penny for anything for the rest of his life.

So the car had no tax or insurance. In addition, he parked it where he felt like parking it and had accumulated hundreds of parking fines, which he then refused to pay. The council had then slapped an embargo on the car so that the next time it was stopped or if they could track the car down, they would snatch it.

After he had left, I insured the car but could not tax it because there were years of unpaid tax accrued in his name amounting to hundreds of pounds and it was not worth paying those bills as the car was in his name. I had only just paid for a year's insurance on the car when he snatched it off me. He didn't have it long, however—only a few weeks. He got caught in Malaga and the car was taken from him to cover the debts he owed the council.

Before we parted and for quite a while afterwards, he amassed all the denuncias or writs together of all the corruption charges and together with his lawyer, they took this mountain of paperwork down to the Palacio de Justicia. His lawyer submitted all the denuncias to the courts on his behalf. There was a great deal to be looked at and he had prepared it all with every legal detail possible, including citing every transgression of the law and quoting exactly which law with reference numbers. The local town hall was informed of these proceedings and was running scared.

A New Teaching Job

I was now looking for a more permanent job. I was happy to work with clients at my home, but I had become tired of travelling back and forth long distances to the clinics on the coast. I applied for a job teaching English with a company who specialised in teaching children. As I had completed a teacher training course, although not in English, I got the job. I worked for a pleasant woman who had bought a franchise and there was a lot of work teaching in schools, colleges and nurseries. I had to attend some training sessions and these were run by a woman and her assistant, who had overall management of the company in that area. They were quite frightful with real ego issues, stuffed with their own self-importance, domineering and intimidating.

I had been teaching for some time when the franchise was sold to somebody else, who was not so pleasant. Then Pamela's boyfriend Matthew decided to move over and arrived to live with us in the village. Pamela was due to start university in Granada that autumn and through the summer, they went off and found a flat there. As Matthew was hoping to work and earn some money, I managed to get him work teaching very young children in nurseries. He was extremely good at it and the children adored him. In nurseries, the children barely spoke their own language and so play and games were the best way to teach them.

Not long afterwards, at one of the training sessions which we were obliged to attend, we were informed that we had to be on constant lookout for every opportunity to promote this company and the woman giving the lecture went on then to give us an example. She told us that she had been watching television and had seen that 12 children had arrived from Russia to stay in Spain on holiday, paid for by some charitable organisation because these children were dying. She saw this as a golden opportunity to promote the company, hastily gathered together her materials and 12 T-shirts with the company's logo on and rushed off to the venue. She managed to push herself in and then managed to get herself photographed with these children, proudly handing each child a T-shirt. As the event was going out on the television news, she hoped that the company's logo would be seen on the T-shirts which she had so generously donated. She was very proud of this initiative.

I was so appalled that anyone could stoop so low as to take advantage of dying children in order to promote their company that I wanted to throw all her papers on the floor, stand up, tell her what I thought of her and walk out. The only reason I didn't do so was because Matthew was sitting next to me, and I knew he would lose his job by his connection to me and he needed the work. I should, however, have done so as it would have done her good by deflating her ego in front of a room full of people.

By that evening, I could contain myself no longer and I telephoned her and expressed my dismay at her tactics with these Russian children and told her I found her behaviour unacceptable. She blustered her reasons. The following day, she and her assistant arrived at one of my classes to 'inspect' me. They sat at the back of the class both dressed in black with faces like thunder, glaring at me the whole time. After the class, they both questioned me intently, trying their best to humiliate me and then fired me. The following day, they fired Matthew for no reason whatsoever but his connection to me. He was in the street at the time when the franchise holder informed him, and he took off his company T-shirt and handed it back to the woman and said she could have the clothes off his back and walked off naked to the waist.

It was a shame for him; he was doing really well and the children loved him. He took the opportunity of moving full time to Granada to be with my daughter, where Pamela was doing her degree, as he had been working 3 days on the coast and spending the rest of the week there. Although my speaking out had caused us to be both fired, it was a blessing in disguise for us both. He was much happier spending the entire week in Granada, and I was delighted to get away from the sorcerer and her apprentice.

Lots of the children and their parents thankfully also loved me too and in a couple of weeks, I was fully booked with private classes, one to one, plus groups of 2, 3, 4 and 5 children and also a few adults. One nursery where I had been teaching cancelled the company and employed me privately and even though the company sent her threatening letters, there was nothing they could do about it. She and I had become good friends, and she had not liked the way they had treated me. It was great to be free of the tightly controlled and restrictive method of teaching and I am always better suited working for myself. A well-stocked language book shop in Malaga provided me with all the books I needed. I developed my own way of teaching and prepared my own teaching aids. There was still pressure, as some of the parents were very anxious that their children did extremely well in English and they certainly had to pass their school exams at very high levels. I enjoyed the classes very much and made many friends.

My first classes were in the mornings in a nursery with children from the age of 2 years old. Some of these children weren't even speaking their own language! It was more like teaching a class of jumping beans and it all had to be done with games, songs, and music. It was pretty exhausting trying to keep them all amused. After a while, before Matthew moved to Granada, I handed over a couple of these classes to him to give him some work and he would stagger out afterwards and head for the nearest bar for a drink to recover. Classes continued all day and went on throughout the evening, I would arrive home at about 10.30 p.m. most evenings.

One class I had was a group of 7 boys aged about 5 and I ran the class in a small hall. They were delightful and very naughty; they really wanted to play football instead of learning English. They got on very well, however, and the end of term session was always attended by the parents to see how they were doing. At one of these events, one 5-year-old bravely stood up and sang the song 'Polly put the Kettle on' perfectly all the way through, and it brought tears to my eyes.

At that venue I got robbed. My car was parked directly outside the door on the street and one time I briefly went to the car which was a yard from the door, got out some papers and in those few moments, someone entered the room and took the equivalent of about £30 from my purse. I discovered the money missing later and when I asked the children if they had seen anybody, they described a young gypsy I had seen hanging around, I was amazed that he could have been so quick without me seeing him. I saw him the next time lurking about and he knew that I was watching him.

It was interesting for me to work in private houses and apartments away from those I knew in my village and to get a glimpse of how different people lived in large towns near and on the coast, such as Velez Malaga and Torre del Mar. It was another world to me and a more normal one where people had orderly homes and gardens. They were professional people, doctors, nurses, teachers and people with their own businesses. The treatment of animals was somewhat better and although nobody seemed to own cats and they were still thrown away and left to starve, several people had dogs and they were very well cared for. One family had even had a special trailer built for their dog to travel in behind their car. I often used to relate tales of the goings on in our village, the fight I was involved in, the corruption of the mayor and town hall and the cruelty to the animals, and these people were genuinely horrified. Most of them had never even ventured inland and one family said they thought everyone a few miles in from the coast were all savages! Many urged me to move at the earliest opportunity.

I taught English at a lot of venues in Velez Malaga, a working town with a lot of character which I loved. One of the classes was with a delightful family for two young children about 6 and 7 years old in a newly built villa, which was part of two new streets built alongside an old settlement of very small cottages, approached by a road with ugly wasteland each side, littered with rubbish. The whole area was a shambles, although these new houses were very pleasant. Whilst I was teaching in this area, a couple who lived in one of the tiny cottages won several millions in the lottery. The lady made tortilla and sold it on her doorstep and continued to do so for some time after the win.

They then had a house built behind this row of cottages which was just enormous. They built it on an elevated piece of ground, it was a beautiful mansion with elaborate adornments and dozens of steps leading up to the front door, about 9 bedrooms and 9 bathrooms. It looked to be a fascinating house enclosed on all sides with huge walls but its position made it look incongruous, surrounded as it was with old houses. I guess they wanted to stay in the very same place where they had always lived, near to their four grown up children. They were well into their sixties by this time. It was certainly quite a landmark in the area, and I took pleasure in taking my visitors up to see it and hearing them gasp as we rounded the corner.

Friend Rick

Around this time when I was working really hard, we became friends with Rick, who we had known for many years. For some extraordinary reason, obviously in a moment of madness, when he was a student learning Spanish at the academy, he decided to buy a derelict little cottage on the edge of a nearby village, the Village from Hell. I would wait there to collect Pamela from the school bus. It is full of rubbish, filth, squalor, starving cats and dead goats and was truly one of the worst places I had ever seen.

At the entrance was a large wooden building housing around 1000 goats for milking. All the excrement oozed out and down onto what was the main track through the village and out the other side. This track, clinging to the side of the goat house like a mantelpiece, was nothing more than a precarious ledge which one had to manoeuvre around in the car, desperately trying not to fall over the edge and plunge down into the river bed whilst sliding on this shit sludge, as well as trying not to run over cats, kittens, skinny dogs or stray goats. The track then led on through hills to a further village and then onto the coast and was a great short cut, cutting miles from a journey to that end of the coast. Driving through the river bed and avoiding this shelf track and some of the village had been a much better option, but after very heavy rainfall, this way was littered with huge rocks and utterly impassable.

That way too had been hazardous enough. On many occasions when the river was full and flowing, several cars would end up abandoned in the water. On the way one morning with Pamela and her friend Oscar in the car, the track had been blocked and the only route through was the river bed. The water was quite deep but feeling confident in a 4 wheel drive Nissan Patrol, I wasn't prepared for the huge hole we suddenly fell into. The car lurched forwards and stalled, the front of the car went down and water came right up over the bonnet to the windscreen. "Oh my God, this is it," I thought, "I've just ruined the engine."

My daughter's thoughts, at the time, she later told me were, "Oh my God, my £50 trainers will be ruined." I put the car into 4 wheel drive, and the car started immediately and hauled us up, reversing out like a digger. I have never been so impressed in my life with any car. I then had to reverse up and out of the river bed and back onto the track and wait for it to clear.

When a goat died and with so many, this was a common occurrence, the farmer threw it into the river bed next to the small bridge leading into the village and along with old mattresses, armchairs, beds and junk of all description, this built up into a huge pile of rotting, stinking, putrid waste which permeated the entire area. Added to this, all the pee and poo from the goat house leaked into the village water supply and flowed down the slope into the river bed.

For some years, Rick had been coming over for holidays and rebuilding his little house until one day, when it was habitable, he decided to leave his job as an art therapist in Berlin and move into the goat village. The first morning of his new life he woke up, opened his front door and looked out on to some waste land opposite and saw someone burning a massive pile of black plastic, belching out huge clouds of foul toxic smoke, which was pouring into his house. He rushed over to the man responsible waving his arms in horror and telling him to stop immediately, as best he could with very little knowledge of the language. Needless to say, his neighbour wasn't impressed, took no notice and worse still, the following morning, Rick got up, wandered outside and discovered that in retaliation for daring to complain so angrily, all his plants had been cut down to ground level—all his geraniums and flowering shrubs which he had been nurturing for years beheaded and scattered all over the place.

He was so horrified by the events, he realised he had made a terrible mistake and packed his bags and went to the airport and got the first flight back to Berlin. After several months, he decided to try again and returned. I often saw him as I was constantly driving past his house to get to work or pick up Pamela, and we started to invite each other round for a drink or a meal. He was looking for work but as he couldn't speak much of the language, it was extremely difficult. I could have got him work on the coast teaching German, there was some interest, but as he couldn't speak Spanish, he was unable to communicate with anybody.

He then went away for a while to Finland where he had a child, and from there we received postcards expressing sweet romantic intentions towards me. I however, was busy working all hours, including every evening, and so when he started complaining that I was too busy to see him, I realised this wasn't going to work. I was so grateful to have such a lot of well-paid work which I loved; I wasn't about to throw it all over for anyone.

Pamela Becomes Gravely Ill

One Christmas whilst Pamela was still in college, she returned to the UK to stay with her father for about 2 weeks during the holidays and was very unwell there, thinking she had the flu. When she returned to Spain, it appeared that she had in fact a bad dose of flu, a very high temperature and feeling very ill. Nothing we did appeared to help and she got worse, with a raging temperature and was very ill in bed. I called a doctor late at night, who came up the mountain from the coast and told me to take her into hospital straight away. A friend came with me and we arrived very late at night. She was put in a wheelchair and taken off for tests. The news was very bad indeed. She was gravely ill. The doctor attending her was in fact the father of two lovely children I was teaching English to in their home and I knew him. He took me to one side and told me that instead of having 200,000 white blood corpuscles in her body, she had 40. Any slight infection would kill her.

He did not know at that time what was wrong with her. I was told there was nothing I could do, and he told me to go home, it was about 1 a.m. I wanted to stay but had to take my friend home.

I have never been in such a bad state, I spent the next few hours on my knees praying for her and at first light, I was back in the hospital. I told him I was a healer and asked permission to give her non-stop healing all day and he was happy about that. They had done some tests and he told me that it was not leukaemia, but they did not know what it was. It was now Saturday and further blood tests could not be carried out until the Monday. He however, strongly suspected it was leishmania, as they called it there, and he started drug treatment for this disease immediately, even before the blood results were confirmed. She was given a great deal of tests and X-rays and on the Monday, it was confirmed that the doctor was right.

Leishmania is an extremely rare disease in Spain in humans, rarer even than leprosy. It is transmitted from an affected dog which is bitten by a sand fly, which then bites a human. Geraldo had a thin dog at that time and had it checked at the vet and it was confirmed with leishmania; he had it put down. However, there are a great many dogs with this disease in Spain, because they are kept outside and it is especially dangerous to leave them out at night. Vets there are dealing with a lot of it. We do not have this disease in England.

Pamela was put into an isolated room and everybody who attended her had to wear a mask, including myself. Apart from the doctors and nurses, I was the only person allowed to enter the room, and there was a clear notice on the door prohibiting anyone to enter.

A couple of days afterwards, there was a very unpleasant and frightening incident. A woman in the village whose child I was teaching English telephoned me and caught me at home on a flying visit to see to the animals, she wanted to know how Pamela was as she had heard all about it. She was very fond of her and they used to chat quite a lot. She paid me a pittance for teaching her daughter and refused to pay me any more. I was earning 4 times as much elsewhere, but I continued for the child's sake. She told me she had flu and I could hear it in her voice.

The next day at the hospital, I had just been down to the restaurant to get some food and I got back to Pamela's room to discover this woman inside her room talking to her. I was very angry and upset and told her to get out immediately. I pointed to the notice on the door and asked her what the hell she thought she was doing, entering the room when it was clearly marked that she couldn't. It also clearly stated that all staff had to wear masks. I was utterly furious, I told her that with the flu she had, she could have given Pamela an infection which would then kill her. I then burst into floods of crying and her husband held me in his arms until I calmed down while she flounced off in a huff without even apologising. They both left and she never spoke to either of us again.

One time, returning to the hospital on a dirt back road which was quicker, I was fairly tanking along as I hated to be away from Pamela, and I flew round a bend not expecting to meet anybody and collided with the school bus. We all piled out and the driver was very sweet, he knew us, our children were friends and he knew what had happened and where I was going. He was one good mayor of a nearby village. I was far too distraught to deal with insurance claims and we both had bangs. He told me to forget it and be on my way and gave me a big smile. I apologised profusely as it was entirely my fault and I was on my way.

I had telephoned home and told the family to come as she was gravely ill. Jack, Sandra and Pamela's boyfriend Matthew all arrived at Malaga airport as soon as they possibly could, within a couple of days, and I picked them up. Pamela had met up with Matthew, her brother's closest friend of many years, on one of her trips home to Somerset and they had become an item. Will was in Hong Kong at the time and just could not get back. They all received a bad shock when they saw her, she was covered in drips and very poorly. Matthew was so shocked, he was unable to speak for an hour or so. I spent the whole time at the hospital. When the family arrived, I did leave her for a while to fit in a few of my classes where children lived near the hospital. I cancelled the rest. She was in hospital for several weeks and gradually got better.

I have since heard of cases of leishmania where foreign tourists have returned to their home countries with this disease and it has taken a long time to work out what on earth is wrong with them. I heard of a case of an Englishman who went from one hospital to another and nobody could find out what was wrong with him. After 2 years and having lost several stone and almost at death's door, he was admitted to the hospital for tropical diseases in London and he was finally diagnosed correctly. I do not know if he survived. I am very deeply grateful that Pamela in fact did not go to the doctor in England before she returned to Spain, as her boyfriend had been urging her to do. I am also deeply grateful that the doctor in charge was able to treat her so successfully. There had only been one case of leishmania in a human in that hospital in its history, but he remembered it and remembered the symptoms.

I believe that the sand fly could well have entered via a gap in the mosquito netting at her bedroom window; this overlooked the garden where Geraldo kept his dogs. In fact when it was checked, all his dogs had the disease.

The people in the village were very kind and supportive and visited me when I returned home briefly from the hospital. Some would wait for me or see me arrive, even though it was a flying visit, many people brought Pamela presents and even my old friend who had chosen to physically and verbally abuse me in the square some years before came to my door to enquire how she was.

The shock of her illness affected me deeply and it also changed me. I have never since been affected by trivialities and for a long time I was in a very strange state of calm. It is when we are faced with something truly serious that we realise what petty things can worry us and I determined then that never again would I ever care about insignificant problems. I have also found that since then, I have no patience with people who make a fuss about small matters, I've had people around me obsessing for months about new kitchen furniture, arguing about their floor tiles, having hysterics about spilt wine, having breakdowns about dents in their cars, being obsessed about tidiness, whinging about every kind of trifling difficulty. I cannot tolerate it.

Shortly after Pamela came home, there was a huge fuss going on in the street and lots of shouting. Two of my neighbours, a mother and daughter, were hysterical, our horse had galloped off over the hills with their mule and they stood there screaming at me. In my new state of utter calm, I just looked at them and didn't speak, I let them rant on and on and let's face it, some of these women can rant for the universe when they get going, and I finally smiled and said, "So what! Let's hope they both enjoy themselves!"

Unfortunately, this outraged them even more and I had to set off to look for them. We found them after a couple of hours, perfectly OK, I am sure the two animals had had a wonderful time together.

After Pamela had recovered, we received a bill for something like £3,500 for her treatment and it was with great relief that on discussing it with the owner of one of the nurseries where I taught, this lady then made enquiries and introduced me to the principal of the college Pamela attended, who told me we were covered by insurance for the pupils.

I was so overcome with relief and gratitude that Pamela had recovered that I offered my services to the hospital as a voluntary interpreter. I had spent so much time there, I had got to know many people, I regularly saw several parents of children I was teaching who worked there. I got to know the restaurant staff too as I had been eating there and the food was delicious. So I spent some time during the following summer holidays, a couple of days a week, when I wasn't required for lessons, translating in the hospital and I thoroughly enjoyed it.

There was a group of us working shifts; usually two of us on at any given time, translating different languages, there were quite a number of tourists who ended up in hospital and also residents who did not speak Spanish. I was mostly called on to interpret for English people, but sometimes for other nationalities who could speak English and not Spanish, such as Germans and Danes. It was very interesting indeed, and it certainly stretched my Spanish. I did a lot of studying in the evenings to make sure I had as much medical information as possible. It helped that I was already a professional therapist and had been discussing medical problems for several years.

There were some funny incidents. One day, I was called by a young handsome doctor who was very frustrated. He told me he spoke English very well but could not understand a word this particular lady was saying. It turned out she was Scottish and was saying things that even I didn't understand. We had a good laugh about it, and I got her to explain carefully and we all managed eventually to understand each other. When I wasn't needed, with the buzzer in my pocket at the ready, I wandered around giving comfort to people, chatting and so on; it felt good to give something back to the hospital that had saved my daughter's life.

I learned a valuable lesson there on the use of the words tu and Usted, meaning you, which can often be confusing. I had been taught that tu was normally used for someone you know very well or a very young person or child, and Usted is used for anyone else. Having spent so much time in the hospital canteen, I had had many chats with one particular guy aged about 35 who served me and always asked me how Pamela was doing.

One day I called him Usted and he became very offended, his face changed and he sarcastically and pointedly then called me Usted back. I apologised and explained that I hadn't realised it would be OK for me to address him as tu. From that point on, I decided to address everybody everywhere as tu, except for very old ladies who I didn't know. I didn't want to risk offending anyone again and decided if anybody got miffed about my being too personal, too bad! On discussing it with my friend Antonio, I discovered that even Spanish people weren't always sure which one to use!

We also discovered after Pamela had recovered that our own boxer dog had contracted leishmania and we took him to the vet and embarked on regular treatment for him. He lived until he was 14 and a half despite this illness and had already recovered from a very serious setback earlier. I had got up one morning to discover him walking about the house banging into the furniture; he appeared to be blind. I rushed him to the vet, who confirmed that he had heart worms; he gave him an injection and one of his eyes returned to normal but the other one remained blind. None of these problems slowed him down in the least. He still ran about and loved long walks on the beach especially.

Heart worms need to be prevented and dogs need to take a tablet daily as it is a very common illness. I hadn't known that.

Pamela at University

Pamela had now recovered completely and she and Matthew were well established in Granada. They had found a small but perfectly located flat right next to a beautiful park in the centre of town and Pamela could walk to University. The park was full of shrubs and flowers and had a stunning fountain where the water changed into different colours every evening. She was working very hard and studying a daunting array of subjects. Her studies included Italian, French, Spanish language and literature, Spanish specialised translation, German specialised translation, advanced English linguistics and Phonetics, German language, Accounting, Economics, Organisations and their Environment, Web Development and Systems Methodologies.

She had taken and passed her entrance examination and had A levels in Latin, Ancient Greek, Spanish language and Spanish literature, Philosophy, French and history. She ended up with a 2.1 BA degree in Spanish, German and Information Systems. Not bad, I need not have had such fears of her trekking up the goat track to a remote village school after all.

I fell utterly in love with Granada, a spectacular city, not only because of the Alhambra, the beautiful ancient Moorish palace, but the enchantment of the Albaicin, the backstreet area of tiny narrow cobbled streets stepped and cascading down a hill and dotted with minute dolls house squares with spectacular views of the palace. There was a delightful street full of Moroccan tea shops, la Calle de las Teterias, huge linking cobbled squares full of flowers and restaurants to sit outside, stunning buildings and churches and the magical backdrop of snow in winter on the mountains behind where one could ski.

After Pamela left, I became intensely lonely and missed her so much that I was in severe pain. I had never known what the empty nest syndrome was, but now I knew in full force. I saw them every weekend, alternately with me going to Granada and them coming back to me. I would pick them up from the bus after I had finished work and we headed for the best fish restaurant in Torre del Mar and treated ourselves to a feast of mixed fried fish and aubergines and local wines, a great way to start the weekend. I certainly looked forward to my weekends in Granada exploring. However, my life now seemed to have taken a turn where I had no idea what to do next. I was happy to keep working and together with her father, we were helping Pamela through university. It was very fortunate that I then met a delightful lady and we began to work together in and around Malaga. I documented this work in my book Divine Communication.

Back to the Colour Green

Throughout the year that Pamela was at university, we had to discuss what our future held and we both decided that at the end of that first year, we would both return to the UK. All I wanted at that point in my life was that my entire family should all live at least in the same country. I could no longer bear the pain of us all living in three different countries, it was driving me crazy. I hadn't given birth and brought up 3 children to then find myself crying for hours on end because I didn't see them and missed them all so much. Will had decided that he too would be returning to England around the same time, so my dream looked promising. Besides, I was tired of the endless struggle in the village, fighting the awful man running it and now without Geraldo, I was alone in that respect. The magic of the Andalucían Mountains had vanished. The many aspects of the harsh reality had set in and I could no longer stomach it.

In addition, there were now new problems regarding the ancient pathways, called la via pecuaria, and I had the local authorities in Malaga breathing down my neck suggesting that one of these pathways may be going through my land. Surveys were being planned to make new and thorough maps in the whole region. More visits to the lawyer, more worry. I was tired of it all, tired of the lack of courage of the people around me to even fight for decency and honesty, half of them being involved in trying to rob anybody they could anyway. The fear and arse-licking of most of the rest of them was becoming nauseating.

The house went on the market in all the local estate agents along the coast. I had a lot of stuff fixed in the house, cracks mended, roof tiles checked, painting, etc. In the March of 1997, Jack and Sandra came and collected Tammy in the horse box and took her back to England and found some great stables nearby for her. In May, Pamela's boyfriend Matthew and I packed up a small Citroen I was driving, loaded up the dog, the 4 remaining cats we had, all my photos and jewellery, a few clothes and we left and drove back to England. It took us 3 days, constantly stopping to deal with the animals.

I had wanted to smuggle the animals in via a yacht to southern Ireland, other people had done it. I had heard of many such cases, Matthew was willing to help me but when both my daughters found out, they nearly had a fit and insisted we do no such thing, so the poor animals were cooped up in quarantine kennels for 6 months, which I never did agree with. They all survived well, although it nearly broke my heart and it cost me a great deal in both money and emotion.

Sandra was waiting for me and with great joy; I followed her high up into the hills of Devon to a sweet enchanting village. Seeing her only once a year had been horrible and those heart-breaking farewells at airports in floods of tears were a thing of the past. Matthew returned to Granada and he and Pamela both came back to England at the end of the first university year in the summer. Jack and I picked up Will from Heathrow, where he had flown in from Kuala Lumpur the same summer. We were all back in England. I was so happy and grateful that my family were at last all together in the same country.

What I noticed so vividly on the first day in Devon was the absolute absence of starving and dying cats and dogs, all I saw were big fat cats and healthy dogs on leads. No more partridges in tiny cages hanging outside so many homes, in a minute space where they could not move, being fattened up for dinner. The second day home, I saw a TV programme where a guy had camped in a bush for 2 days and nights waiting for the sighting of a kingfisher to land on a piece of string he had rigged up over a stream and when he finally saw it, he was beside himself with excitement. I was overcome with emotion. I was home. This was where I belong.

It took 4 years to sell the house. When I finally found a purchaser, I flew over to Spain with the flu, barely able to stand up. An hour before we were due to go to the notary to sign the papers, the mayor arrived to inform the would be purchasers that the land with my house belonged to him. They naturally backed out. I tried to explain to them the situation and what a bastard he was but they didn't believe me. I was naturally very upset but decided it was meant to be and took it as calmly as I could—what else could I do? Hire a hit man from Ronnie Knight? What I did was realise that with him in charge, I may never sell the place and my kids would have to sort it out when I was gone.

When I did finally sell it, I had to fly to Spain 6 times during a period of 6 months, on one occasion 10 days after I had just got back to UK. The paperwork was unbelievable. The Escritura still had written on it that the house was in ruins, I hadn't known it had to be changed at the land registry office after the building work was complete. I had to employ an architect and get all the plans done again, this time according to new regulations which were now much stricter. I had to get signatures from my friend the mayor, who took great delight in all the problems I was experiencing. I had to find the original permission from the town hall from 1983, a piece of paper about 3 inches x 4 inches.

In addition, the notary wanted bank statements back to 1983 which the bank in Madrid had in their vaults and I had to wait some weeks to receive them. When I finally presented them to the notary, having had to return to the UK in the meantime as I had a full time job, he sheepishly said they didn't really matter after all. Then on another occasion, I was told to arrive on a certain day by the gestor dealing with the sale, but when I flew out, their papers weren't ready after all and I had to return to the UK and go back 10 days later. That time, I presented them with the bill for my airfare.

To say it was a nightmare, is an understatement and as I write, I am still waiting for the return of monies paid to the government at the time of the sale, which they are supposed to return to you but the reality is they will find every excuse in the book not to do so. Organising the removal of all my furniture and belongings which were all still in the house was another drama, having gone to a crook who was pretending to be a member of staff in the company who had originally moved us to Spain. He took my money and left half the stuff behind so I had to get yet another removal company to bring the rest.

Some Final Justice

Needless to say, the tortoise-like speed and inefficiency in the overwhelmed justice system didn't get round to putting the mayor in jail. However, fortunately, the people in my village eventually found the courage to do something about their diabolical dictator. They formed a separate independent political party, headed up by the postman, a delightful man, the leader of the opposition, and got everybody outside the mayor's family, to vote for him and at last, after 28 years of tyranny, the bastard was out. They had all previously been too scared to vote for anybody else for fear of reprisals. The joy when I heard the news made me leap and dance round the house, whooping and screaming with delight.

The mayor is now out of work and has sunk into a deep state of depression and is being consoled by the priest. It was claimed that the village priest was found abusing very many young boys and despite protests and petitions, managed to hang on to his job. The mayor's wife has had to return to normal life, instead of swanning round like a queen bee. She even has to work on the roads mixing cement again each year for two weeks in order to earn her unemployment benefit. Not long ago, the mayor, suffering from delusions of grandeur and self-pity, and no doubt a lack of ready cash, and apparently having believed he was going to be mayor for life, mounted some kind of legal battle/coup and tried to have the party thrown out and have himself reinstated. The people actually took to the streets and demonstrated against him, can you imagine? He failed. If this country ever decides to increase the powers of our local mayors such as they have in Europe, heaven help us all.